"Steve's latest book provides an essential developmental tool for all our sales associates."

John McGinty, Chief Customer Officer, Nestlé Purina

"Everything happens in negotiation for a reason. This excellent book explains the negotiation process and how you can secure the best total value. A must-read if you are to be successful."

Ken McKnight, President, CRH Asia

"This is what I have been looking for. An intelligent and pragmatic guide to understanding and developing your negotiation skills in a dynamic and challenging world."

Claire Lenighan, Head of Trader and Supplier
Engagement, Asda Walmart

"*The Negotiation Book* with interesting updated real life examples. Steve and his team from Gap Partnership has over the last 10 years trained over hundreds of my company's executives and has helped to generate of millions of dollars of value. *The Negotiation Book*'s collaborative method of negotiation helps in gaining agreement that not only results in value for all parties involved but also enhances relationships. It emphasizes on the psychological and behavioral aspects of the negotiator, which is the one of the single most important factor in a successful negotiation. I hope that this book will inspire the readers to continually practice and train themselves to become a 'complete skilled negotiator'."

John Lim, General Manager, Supply Chain & Procurement Asia Pacific,
Middle East and Africa, CoconoPhillips

"An unputdownable step-by-step guide to successful negotiations. Essential for business professionals, it offers universally acceptable 'around the clock' negotiation methods supported heavily by easy-to-understand case studies. Very practical."

Poitr Malita, Commercial Capability Director,
Coca-Cola HBC

D0413861

"It just makes sense! If you fully absorb what Steve has to say, you should feel confident and fairly sure of the positive outcome of your negotiation before you even enter the room!"

Simon Duncan, Director of External
Business, House of Fraser

"The concepts and framework presented within this book are invaluable in helping you prepare and execute your negotiation strategy. This negotiation 'blueprint' will ensure that readers have every opportunity to secure long term sustainable agreements with their trade partners."

Martin Porter, Sales Managing Director, Heineken

THE NEGOTIATION BOOK

YOUR DEFINITIVE GUIDE TO SUCCESSFUL NEGOTIATING

Second edition

Steve Gates

CAPSTONE
A Wiley Brand

This edition first published 2016
© 2016 Steve Gates
First edition published 2011 by John Wiley and Sons Ltd

Registered office
John Wiley and Sons Ltd, The Atrium, Southern Gate, Chichester, West Sussex, PO19 8SQ, United Kingdom

For details of our global editorial offices, for customer services and for information about how to apply for permission to reuse the copyright material in this book please see our website at www.wiley.com.

Wiley publishes in a variety of print and electronic formats and by print-on-demand. Some material included with standard print versions of this book may not be included in e-books or in print-on-demand. If this book refers to media such as a CD or DVD that is not included in the version you purchased, you may download this material at http://booksupport.wiley.com. For more information about Wiley products, visit www.wiley.com.

Library of Congress Cataloging-in-Publication Data

Gates, Steve, author.
  The negotiation book : your definitive guide to successful negotiating / Steve Gates. — Second edition.
    pages cm
  Includes index.
  ISBN 978-1-119-15546-1 (pbk.) 1. Negotiation in business.
2. Negotiation in business—Case studies. I. Title.
  HD58.6.G38 2016
  658.4′052—dc23

                                                                    2015025693

A catalogue record for this book is available from the British Library.

ISBN 978-1-119-15546-1 (paperback)
ISBN 978-1-119-15551-5 (ebk)
ISBN 978-1-119-15552-2 (ebk)

Cover design: Wiley

Set in 11.5/15pt Adobe Jenson Pro Regular by Aptara, New Delhi, India
Printed in Great Britain by TJ International Ltd, Padstow, Cornwall, UK

Contents

About the Author

 **Steve Gates** is founder and CEO of The Gap Partnership, the world's leading negotiation consultancy. Since 1997 Steve has consulted with and supported global corporations from all business sectors facing the challenge of optimizing value from their many and varied negotiations. His interest in commerce, capitalism, and psychology continues to inspire his innovative flair and passion for greater insights into the art and science of negotiation. His home remains in the UK.

Acknowledgments

I would like to thank an exceptional team of negotiators from across The Gap Partnership with whom I have shared so many experiences and drawn so much inspiration. They have committed their lives to pushing negotiation capability to a new level, which has allowed me to write this account of the Complete Skilled Negotiator – a philosophy based on the human challenges of negotiating today, which they have all helped build and which serves to inspire our clients around the world, every day.

prescriptive, but aims to help you to get better deals by being aware that it is you who are responsible for making decisions based on your own judgement. The amount of time people actually spend negotiating is very small in the context of their whole job and yet the consequences of their performance during negotiations will often distinguish how successful they are. The art and science of negotiation is an interactivity that is influenced by culture, ever-changing circumstances, expectation, capability, and personal chemistry. The Complete Skilled Negotiator is an individual who has both the skills and mindset to do that which is appropriate to their circumstances and the ability to maximize opportunity during each and every negotiation.

So why this second edition? Well, over the past decade there is not much that has changed about how people and companies negotiate. There has, however, been a rapid change around what they are negotiating over and the value attributed to time, risk, convenience, and information as the benefits of technology are realized in all our lives. I've taken a fresh look at some of these agreements and how, in some industries, information access has become as valuable as payment terms, or response service times as important as contract length. Technology is changing what is possible, what is expected, and what is traded, which is providing a new mix of variables featuring in all types of agreements. More negotiations are being conducted through multiple forms of communication. What used to be face-to-face, telephone, and email negotiations can now include video conferencing from your telephone, meeting rooms from anywhere round the world, online data rooms, online auctions, and the list goes on.

The abilities of the Complete Skilled Negotiator, however, remain the same. They are balanced in their thinking, have their ego in check and are focused on understanding the interests and priorities of the other party. They are chameleon like in their approach, in that they know how to be what they need to be depending on their circumstances, and are not burdened by personal values that wear away at their consciousness. Their ability to read situations, take the time to prepare, and have the capacity to think around the issues, as well as deal with the relationship dynamics at the same time, helps them perform in a confident manner. Most of all, they focus on the potential of the deal rather than trying to win, understanding that being competitive will only serve to attract friction, which is generally counterproductive (unless used for a specific purpose).

It can be the most rewarding of skills to exercise and the most nerve wracking. Is it any wonder that to provide a standard that helps everyone to negotiate more effectively has proved such a challenge to so many in the past? Yet simple disciplines, proactive planning, and a clear, conscious state of mind can provide a significant uplift in what you can achieve.

So what do I mean by a standard? *The Negotiation Book* covers the traits and behaviors associated with the Complete Skilled Negotiator. I use the word complete rather than successful because who are we to judge if your performances are as successful as they might be? We will never know. The standard also refers to a clock face model that provides a way of differentiating the range of ways we negotiate in a dynamic, capitalist market. Importantly it also recognizes that, although the concepts of power, process, and behavior have much to do with performance, so do the psychology, self-discipline, and human interaction that make up the framework. The standard is not here to restrict but to empower you as a Complete Skilled Negotiator to negotiate that which is possible ... given those opportunities you are presented with.

The experience I have gained from practical hands-on involvement in having negotiated with some of the largest corporations on the planet, including P&G, Walmart, Morgan Stanley, Nestlé, GE, and Vodafone, has helped me to provide this account of the standard that has been adopted in the business world. I have also been privileged to work with dozens of highly skilled negotiation practitioners at The Gap Partnership who have negotiated with, advised, and developed hundreds of such organizations globally. It is this experience that has helped us to crystallize what our clients have come to call "the standard" for negotiating.

I am about to share with you a way of thinking, behaving, and performing, together with a standard for doing so. There is no magic formula or magic wand, but there are principles that will help you to secure agreements with others who may not always see the world the way you do. This book is about *you* gaining more value from every agreement you're involved in, understanding what to do, when to do it and, most importantly, providing you with the inspiration to do it.

CHAPTER 1

So You Think You Can Negotiate?

"It is what we know already that often prevents us from learning."
Claude Bernard

SO WHAT IS NEGOTIATION?

Negotiation is a necessity, a process, and an art. It evokes complex feelings that many seek to avoid and yet it is fundamental to how business gets done and takes place millions of times a day around the world. If you can take control of yourself, your values and prejudices, your need for fairness, and your ego, you may start to realize the best possible outcomes in your negotiations. The biggest challenge here is not in educating you in how to be a better negotiator, but motivating you to change the way you think about negotiations and yourself. Of the many thousands of negotiation workshops I have provided at The Gap Partnership, the greatest change I see clients make is that of self-awareness. Learning about negotiation is an exercise in self-awareness because understanding yourself and what effect a negotiation can have on you, enables you to accommodate the pressures, dilemmas, and stresses that go with it. Self-awareness helps us to recognize why we do the things we do and the effect this has on our results. It also helps us adapt our approach and our behavior to suit each negotiation rather than trying to make one approach fit every situation, simply because it suits our personal style.

Why bother negotiating?

Just because everything is negotiable doesn't mean that everything has to be negotiated. The value of your time versus the potential benefit that can be achieved by negotiating is always a consideration. Why spend ten minutes negotiating over the price of a $10 notebook when you normally make $100 an hour? So you may save $2 – that's 20 cents a minute! However, if it is your next car and a 5% saving could equate to $1500, the time is probably worth investing.

There will be situations involving more important decisions where you are mutually dependent and yet hold different views. When an agreement needs working through, effective negotiation can help provide not only a solution but potentially a solution that both of you are motivated to carry through.

volume threshold
This term is used to determine a level at which benefits such as pricing, discounts, delivery, or other services become applicable.

There is no other skill set that can have such an immediate and measurable level of impact on your bottom line than negotiation. A small adjustment to the payment terms, the specification, the **volume threshold**, or even the delivery date will all impact on the value or profitability of the agreement.

Understanding the effects of these moves, and the values they represent to you from the outset, is why planning is fundamental to effective negotiation. The skill in building enhanced agreements through trading off against different interests, values, and priorities is negotiation. In the business context it is known as the skill of profit maximization.

So, effective negotiation provides the opportunity to build or dissolve value – but what does value *really* mean? It can be too easy and is too often a focus on price. The question of "how much?" is one, transparent, measurable issue and, because of this, is also the most contentious issue in the majority of negotiations.

Yet price is but *one* **variable** you can negotiate over. It *is* possible to get a great price and feel as though you have won and yet get a very poor deal at the same time. For example, because the item did not arrive on time, or it fell apart after being used twice, or it had no flexibility about it, and so on. (Ever heard the saying "you get what you pay for"?)

variable

This can be a price or any term of condition that needs to be agreed.

In negotiation, your ego and your competitiveness might fuel the need to "win," especially where you allow a sense of competition to become involved. However, negotiating agreements is not about competing or winning; it is about securing the best value. This means understanding:

- what the other person or party wants, needs or believes;
- what they do; and
- how that affects the possibilities.

pressure points

Pressure points are things, times or circumstances which influence the other party's position of power.

As a Complete Skilled Negotiator your focus needs to be on what is important to the other party: *their* interests, priorities, options, if any, their deadlines, and their **pressure points**. Try to see the deal as they see it. If you set out to understand them and their motivations, you may be able to use these insights to your advantage and, ultimately, increase the value of the deal for yourself. Being driven to beat the other party will distract you from your main objective, which is usually to maximize value from the agreement.

Proactivity and control

Your first task is to be proactive – to take control of the way you negotiate. To map out the issues, formulate an agenda which helps you to negotiate agreement in a way that will serve your objectives. Try to be honest with yourself when deciding or agreeing on what these are. Remember, *price is only one element of the deal* and winning on price may not result in your attracting the best deal. You may need cooperation to the point where the other party not only agrees to go ahead but is also prepared to *honor* their commitment. There is absolutely no place for your ego in your negotiations. The single thing that matters is the **total value** over the life time of the agreement.

Becoming comfortable with being uncomfortable

The person on the other side of the negotiating table may well take up a tough position, which could make you feel challenged or even competitive. Becoming *more* comfortable with being uncomfortable in situations like this, where you are also likely to experience pressure and tension is one of the most important prerequisites of a skilled negotiator. Without this, our ability to think and perform can become compromised. So you need to recognize that, by negotiating, you are involved in a process and the people you negotiate with need time to adjust as part of engaging in this process. Typically this is when:

- any new risks, obligations, conditions, or consequences are presented; and
- any new proposals that you make, which materially change the value of the agreement.

EMPOWERED, INEXPERIENCED NEGOTIATORS REPRESENT A REAL RISK

The adoption of cloud-based technology solutions into organizations has created a fast-changing, complex environment where it's important not only to have technology specialists on your side, but a negotiator who can make sense of the variables featured in contracts.

PIC, a Paris-based consultancy business, were keen to invest in a new HR management system to help manage the challenges around managing their ever growing team. During their research they identified a solution which also offered an integrated Learning Management Systems (LMS). This is a platform for managing staff development and also houses content for training purposes that staff can access.

People Technologies, the potential supplier, made a compelling pitch to PIC on the basis that their LMS system might also be used as a platform for servicing PIC's own clients. This meant that PIC would acquire not only a system that serviced its own business but a solution which could extend their service offering to their own clients.

The newly appointed technology manager sold the idea to the board of PIC who were impressed with his creative thinking. The annual license fee was twice the budget allocation but the client-facing provision was sold as a real opportunity to "provide a monetized technology solution to its clients," won the board over.

The board bought the idea and signed a 3-year contract. However, it soon became apparent that the venture was a first for People Technologies. Although a large business, it had never provided its service to a client as a resale facility. There were issues that had not been thought through, such as chargeable licensing and the fact that PIC would be liable for every one of its client users. Issues around integration and maintenance had not been fully understood or negotiated by the technology manager. The board had assumed his understanding of the interdependencies. Within weeks, the CFO having faced questions from the operations team investigated the implications of the contract and realized that the opportunity lacked coherence. It subsequently cost the company half the cost of the 3-year contract to exit and the technology manager his job.

So, even though the board had committed to a solution for twice the cost of their budget on the basis of it serving other client-based services, the ill suited solution had to be abandoned within months.

In business meetings, people can become frustrated, emotional, and upset if they feel that you are simply being irrational or unfair with your proposals. Some will even walk away before considering the consequences.

For this reason, the more experienced the negotiator you are working with, the less chance you will have of a deadlocked conversation. They are more likely to understand that they are involved in a process and that nothing is agreed until everything is agreed and sometimes the process can be frustrating. In fact, their experience can result in you attracting a better deal than when you negotiate with an untrained negotiator. Many of my clients insist that their suppliers attend the same training in negotiation as they do, as part of ensuring that both parties work towards maximizing total value rather than becoming distracted by short-term gains and/or trying to "win".

THE NEED FOR SATISFACTION

Everyone likes to secure a bargain; to buy something at a better price than was available before. You only have to visit department stores on December 27 to witness the effect that securing a bargain can have on people's behavior. Such can be the frenzy that it is not unknown for violence to be used where one person feels another has pushed ahead of them in the queue. Many people just can't help themselves when there's a good bargain to be had. In extreme cases people will buy things they don't want or even need if the price is right.

In business, though, what is the right price? The answer depends on a whole range of other issues, which, of course, need to be negotiated. So how do you manage the other party's need for satisfaction? That is, their natural need to feel as though they got a better deal than was originally available.

- Do you start out with an extreme opening on price?
- Do you introduce conditions that you are ready to concede on?
- Do you build in red herrings (issues that are not real, that you can easily, and you expect to, concede)?

The psychological challenge here is to provide the other party with the satisfaction of having achieved, through hard work, a great deal for *themselves*. In other words letting them "win," or letting them have *your* way.

Negotiating versus selling

It is a commonly held view that a good "sale" will close itself and that negotiation follows only when outstanding differences remain. However, negotiation as a skill and as a process is fundamentally different from selling. To sell is to promote the positives, the match, to align the solution to the need. It requires explanation, justification, and a rational case. "The gift of the gab" is associated with the salesman who has an enthusiastic answer for everything. Negotiation does not. Although relationships can be important, as is the climate for cooperation (without which you have no discussion), the behavior of the Complete Skilled Negotiator also involves **silence**, where appropriate. That means listening to everything the other party is saying, understanding everything they are not saying, and working out their true position.

silence
Silence offers you the time to think and contemplate before responding. It allows you to listen to the other party to really understand. It requires discipline and concentration. The unnerving consequence of silence is that the other party continues to talk and ultimately make unplanned concessions. At the very least they often provide you with more information than they intended.

Negotiation involves planning, questioning, listening, and making proposals, but it also requires you to recognize when the selling has effectively concluded and the negotiation has begun. If you find yourself selling the benefits of your proposals during a negotiation, you are demonstrating a weakness and probably giving away power. It suggests that you don't feel that your proposals are strong enough and that they require further promoting. The more you talk, the more you are likely to make a concession.

So, recognizing when the change from selling to negotiating has taken place is critical. You are now negotiating. It is simple enough to shut up, listen, and think, whilst exercising patience. If this silence feels uncomfortable, it is; because you are now negotiating.

PERSONAL VALUES

Values such as fairness, integrity, honesty, and trust naturally encourage us to be open. Personal values have their place within any relationship but business relationships can and often do exist, based on different value sets.

Values are usually deep-rooted and many people feel very defensive about them, as if their very integrity was being challenged. The point here is that they are not right or wrong. I am not suggesting that effective negotiators have no values – we all do. However, in negotiation, when you are involved in a process, what you *do* and what you *are* need not be the same thing. This is not about challenging who you are, but it is about helping you to change the things you *do*.

If you want to remain loyal to your values during negotiation there is nothing wrong with this. However, others may not be as faithful to theirs, which could leave you compromised. In other words, if you choose to be open and honest by, for example, sharing information with the other party and they decide not to reciprocate, guess who will gain the balance of power? And how appropriate is that?

Where natural economic laws, such as supply and demand, result in people doing business with each other, a cooperative relationship can help to create greater opportunities but it is not always critical. Trust and honesty are great corporate values: they are defendable and safe, especially when you have a business involving hundreds or thousands of people buying or selling on behalf of one business. They also help promote sustainable business relationships. However, in a negotiation, these values can be the root of complacency, familiarity, and even lazy attitudes that end up costing shareholders money. I remain a strong believer in collaborative relationships but with the emphasis on optimizing value whilst ensuring the best interests of *all* involved.

The case for collaboration

If you prefer collaborative negotiations it could be because:

- you need the commitment and motivation of the other party in order to deliver on what you have agreed;

- you prefer to work within a range of variables that allow you to consider all of the implications and the total value in play;
- you regard it as a better way of managing relationships; or
- you simply fear conflict and the potential negative consequences of the negotiation breaking down.

Whatever your reason, you should ensure that it is because it's more likely to meet *your objectives* rather than simply a style preference that provides for a comfortable environment. How appropriate this is depends on how honest you are with yourself about your motives and the benefits that collaboration will bring.

HONESTY WITH YOURSELF

It is often difficult to work out how good a deal you really have secured following a negotiation. This would be far easier to work out if, when we reviewed our performance, self-justification was left out of the equation. Have you ever asked yourself: "If I had performed differently or taken different decisions, could I have secured a better deal?" It is easier to move on rather than reflect on our performance and consider the what and the why, and of course the resulting quality of the deal we finished up with. Learning something from each negotiation ensures that, where unplanned compromises have taken place, you take away some value from the experience. This requires honesty with yourself. The following four areas provide a useful frame of reference for review, and as preparation for your next negotiation.

The four challenges we face

Challenge 1: This is all about you

Negotiation is uncomfortable. It sometimes involves silence, threats, and consequences that many find difficult environments to perform well in. If you are to perform well, you will need to accept responsibility for your actions and recognize the significant difference your performance can make to every agreement you are involved in.

The art of negotiation can be learned and applied, but you must have the self-motivation for change and the ability to be flexible. This is not just about being tough or being prepared. It is firstly about being motivated by the prospect of creating value and profit from well-thought-through agreements. You should therefore recognize that your past performance is no indication of your future performance, especially as every negotiation is unique, like every basketball or football game.

So, the first challenge is you. It is *people* who negotiate; not machines, or companies. We all have prejudices, values, ideologies, preferences, pressures, objectives, and judgment, as will the other party in your negotiations. So one part of our journey will involve you understanding why your greatest challenge in negotiation is yourself and how, by nature, you naturally see the world from your perspective rather than that of others.

The simple process of an exploratory meeting, patience, and seeking to work *with* someone rather than to assume and then impose ideas on that person, is key to understanding how others see the world and what their objectives are when you are both selling and negotiating. As an effective negotiator you need to be able to understand the dynamics of any situation from "inside" the other party's head. Without this insight, you will remain in a state that we at The Gap Partnership call "being inside your own head," which is a dangerous place to be during negotiation. If you really want to negotiate effectively, you first have to get your thinking this way round.

UNDERSTANDING THE OPPORTUNITY FROM THEIR PERSPECTIVE

A German electronics firm, ETD, who specialized in Bluetooth technology had built a successful relationship with a number of suppliers to the German auto industry. They had developed software that enabled them to program their "in-car module" to operate with virtually anything Bluetooth-enabled without interference from any other signals. It was a real breakthrough in being able to offer a reliable high-quality solution for those fitting electronics into vehicles. It meant that as well as radio, mobile, and other devices, wiring in vehicles could almost become a thing of the past. The lights on the car, fuel flap, windows, and even ignition could be actioned via this Bluetooth device. Although the electronic hardware was not unique, the software itself was and ETD had set about educating the trade and selling the benefits.

ETD Sales Director Thomas Schnider held a meeting with the procurement team at Brionary, a main components supplier to the auto industry. He presented a carefully planned business case, which justified the premium price point by demonstrating how savings could be made elsewhere as a result of using their software.

ETD understood that this type of change would at best be considered for the next generation of vehicles. Their excitement for this potential prevented them from getting inside the head of the buyers at Brionary. The questions asked by Brionary were:

1. "Can we buy access to the software and program ourselves?"
2. "We purchase most of the electronics through suppliers who we are co-invested in. How can we overcome this challenge?"
3. "How long do you think it will be before this type of software is copied?"

The answer: probably before the next generation of vehicles comes to market.

Thomas and his team retreated to their office in Cologne to reassess their strategy. They had approached the opportunity and the potential to negotiate terms from inside their own head. A month later they offered Brionary access to the software as a concession for a longer-term contract on their existing range of hardware components. Had they been in the heads of Brionary, who clearly had an open mind to long-term co-investment, their approach and the outcome may have been quite different.

Challenge 2: There are no rules

In negotiation there are no rules. No set procedures, no cans or cannots. Negotiation is often likened to a game of chess – the difference being that in most negotiations you are not necessarily trying to beat an opponent, and are not restricted to alternate moves. Although there may be no absolute rules in negotiation, there are parameters within which we can operate. Most negotiators are empowered by their boss to negotiate but only to a certain level, beyond which discussions are usually escalated. Total empowerment results in exposure and risk which for obvious reasons is usually inappropriate.

Challenge 3: Knowing when you have performed well

How will you know how well you have negotiated? You won't, because the other party is unlikely to tell you how you might have done better or how well you performed relative to their other options.

So, without the benefit of feedback from those we negotiate with, we have to rely on previous precedents (the outcome last time round), or absolute measurements (our profit and loss sheet), and have the humility to face such questions as:

- What might I have done differently?
- Might I have timed things differently?
- Might I have included other issues?
- Might I have tabled proposals that were better thought through?
- Might I have not agreed so easily at the end?

Questions like these challenge how honest you are being with yourself. A good deal has to be defined, taking all of the circumstances into account. Our ego can lead us to blame our circumstances when the deal becomes challenged. By the time a deal is done, you may just want to get on with implementation rather than reflect on your performance.

Measuring the quality of your agreement, without acknowledging some of the risks or concessions that have allowed for **the price** to appear like a "good deal," is not measuring the total value, thus failing to provide a true reflection of your performance. It is your honesty in self-review that needs to be encouraged if you are to truly measure the real value of your deals and learn from our performances.

> **the price**
> A single issue which offers only one measure and is usually not representative of the quality or total value of the agreement.

No good, bad, right, or wrong

In negotiation there is no good or bad, right or wrong. The economies we work in are dynamic, as are our suppliers, customers, and competitors. What was a great deal last week may be less well celebrated this week, because our circumstances are continually changing. Negotiation is about doing things that are appropriate to each situation you face with the information as you see it at that moment in time.

Appropriateness

Knowing how a car was built and how it works does not make you a good driver. When driving with so many obstacles on the road, the challenge is to be able to maintain confidence, navigate, interpret, and, where necessary, respond to situations in the most appropriate way when there is no absolute answer that suits all situations.

The same applies to negotiation in business.

- Should you set out to compete or to work with the other party?
- Should you seek to manipulate the situation or collaborate instead?
- Should you trust them or work on being trusted by them?
- How will your options influence the balance of power?
- Is the perception of power and dependency between you and the other party based on reality?

In so many cases the answer is based on *appropriateness*; that is, the ability to adapt and respond, depending on your circumstances. This requires an objective, rational, balanced mindset: a state that few human beings can maintain at all times, especially when faced with degrees of perceived conflict, rejection, and demands, all of which need to be accommodated within the negotiation.

Challenge 4: Nothing happens by accident

The essence of negotiation is doing what is appropriate for your circumstances. This means being conscious of everything that happens before, during, and after your negotiation. In negotiation, nothing happens by accident; everything happens for a reason. Being in control of yourself, your emotions, and the relationship is a critical attribute for a negotiator. The challenge is that these qualities do not, for most of us, come naturally. Effective negotiators develop their awareness to the point that they do not lose touch with the human sensitivities necessary to manage relationships, and that they do not compromise for the sake of personal gratification for their own comfort, or to remove the stress they experience when challenged with the prospect of deadlock.

KEY TAKEAWAYS
- *The Negotiation Book* will provide a you with a thought-provoking insight into the reality of what it will take for you to become the Complete Skilled Negotiator.
- The more you understand tactics, strategies, behaviors, processes, and planning tools, the better prepared you can become.
- Ultimately it is you, and perhaps your team, who will conduct your negotiations; you who will be accountable for your actions and the outcomes; and you who may or may not act on the opportunities before you.
- It is you who will need to manage your relationships, emotions, and the climate that so heavily influences possibility.
- Self-awareness will help you to adapt your approach and your behavior to suit each negotiation rather than trying to make one approach fit every situation.

CHAPTER 2

The Negotiation Clock Face

*"There is no right, no wrong, no good, and no bad way to negotiate.
Only that which is appropriate to your circumstances."*

Steve Gates

To make sense of how different approaches to negotiation could serve us, and because each negotiation presents a unique challenges, I developed a model called the Negotiation Clock Face. This model was born out of a commercial project I undertook to research and explore the many philosophies being advocated by so called gurus, academics, authors, consultancies, and, importantly, the group of organizations that I represented for at that time, to define what is meant by "world class negotiation."

Figure 2.1 The clock face.

The definitions on the right-hand side of the clock face represent competitive negotiations based on those involved distributing a finite amount of value between them. It symbolizes transactional dialogs with lower levels of trust and fewer issues regarded as important enough to negotiate. This means that those on the right are tougher to negotiate in nature and are either win—lose or competitive forms of negotiation. So the process is going to be positional and potentially confrontational. The pie is only so big and it's simply a case of how it gets distributed.

Those definitions on the left-hand side of the clock face provide for more cooperation where collaborative negotiations lead to the creation of incremental value (creating a bigger pie). They reflect negotiations which are more commonly promoted in business-to-business (B2B) situations (though not always). There is more dependency, higher levels of trust and a broader agenda around which to negotiate value.

However, these definitions are only a guide, in that many negotiations move from one area to another in the same meeting. The Complete Skilled Negotiator recognizes this and will move the discussions into the area that suits their objectives, depending on those considerations which are important to them (relationship, sustainability, or, if they choose, short-term value).

The "engineering of variables"

The opportunity to build value through the "engineering of variables" and each party's relationship with the other is more likely to take place where there is collaboration in play, that is, on the left-hand side of the clock. Collaboration of course requires some degree of common purpose, interest, or dependency between those involved. No matter how proactive or committed you are to developing a joint agreement, creating more value opportunities through negotiation requires the commitment of both parties, or such power on one side that the other has no option but to collaborate. Maximizing value through the engineering of variables need not be detrimental to the other party. They remain responsible for their actions and decisions as you remain responsible for yours. However, you should never allow complacency or the idea of fairness to affect your drive for improved terms as you will inevitably face resistance and challenge along the way, however you build your agreements.

The clock face, then, is a model for helping you, to determine what is "appropriate for each of your situations." The clock face in simple terms defines capitalism. One way or another it reflects how most deals "get done". This model was designed to help negotiation practitioners differentiate between negotiations and consciously adopt the appropriate approach to each of their negotiations.

The clock face model is not good or bad, right or wrong, any more than north, south, east, or west is the right direction for any journey. It just "is" and, wherever capitalism exists, the clock face serves to offer a simple range of definitions within which your negotiations will take place. It is important to remember that the direction you take, decisions you make and results you achieve still remain *your* responsibility. The clock face is simply a compass.

WHY ARE THERE SO MANY DIFFERENT WAYS TO NEGOTIATE A DEAL?

Capitalism and market pressures motivate and manipulate people to operate in the ways that they do. For example, account managers frequently become frustrated when trying to build relationships with buyers who they perceive to have more power within the relationship. The buyer (and this often works both ways) will negotiate competitively to drive every last cent of value out of the deal. As a result the buyer can become so focused on one issue that they are prepared to forfeit any other benefits whilst in the pursuit of the best price. Meanwhile, the account manager, desperate to build value through a range of variables (payment terms, volume, quality, delivery, and other offerings), tries to progress conversations on a collaborative basis resulting in proposals which in this case go ignored.

So what is the answer? There is no one answer. How you negotiate will nearly always depend on the specific circumstances you face. This is why, to understand negotiation, you first need a basis for differentiating the many ways in which negotiation can and does take place (the Negotiation

Clock Face). The above situation, however, is certainly manageable. Escalation to a higher authority, introducing more variables onto the agenda, conditional movement from your position, or even introducing time constraints could offer a start.

When asked to describe their preferred negotiation style, many negotiators have openly described to me how they get the best results, the way that best suits their industry, or the way their business does business. The response is rarely "it depends." The importance of relationships or dependency will often feature as the primary motive for preferring collaborative negotiations. This view of how negotiations can best be managed usually results in the individuals being effective in only one type of negotiation or relationship situation. The Complete Skilled Negotiator has a much broader understanding of the options available and is able to adapt to each situation as they find it.

WHEN ONE APPROACH DOES NOT WORK FOR ALL

A contract team working for Collberth, an industrial space management company, were responsible for outsourcing security contracts for over 200 commercial properties (amongst other services). The nature of the locations, occupants, and other factors meant that the precise nature of cover had to be spread across nine different security firms.

Over the years, the team had developed standard practices and systems to support the management of the contracts, which had resulted in them working with a pre-defined set of variables. The team was even incentivized by the board of Collberth on how effective they were at optimizing the terms of each contract.

Nothing unusual here you might think. They were a team that had been in place for 4 years with a deep familiarity with the market. So they started to adopt a growing trend of assumptions around supplier motives. Every contract renewal commenced with a 6-month countdown prior to any contract expiring. A preferred way, a formulaic way, had developed: "the way" to negotiate at Collberth.

In 2014, five of the contracts were up for renewal at different times. Each one in turn deadlocked and not because of changing market conditions. By early 2015 the board intervened to examine the cause behind the change. The contract team quickly defended their position and the contingency actions they had implemented. The findings of the board were that the team had become so inflexible and rigid in their process and attitudes that they had left no scope for interpretation, alternate strategies, or optimizing terms based on the circumstances of what were still highly competitive suppliers.

Although there is no right or wrong way to negotiate an agreement, there is an appropriate way. This will invariably depend on the circumstances of the other party, rather than any set rigid terms that you decide to operate by.

HOW THE NEGOTIATION CLOCK FACE WORKS

The Negotiation Clock Face offers a visual representation of negotiation styles ranging from the toughest form of market manipulation through to high-dependency relationships. Each stage around the clock face offers more complexity, more opportunity, and more collaboration required. It helps us to understand and determine the most appropriate approach to negotiating, depending on your circumstances.

The clock face as a reference point, therefore, helps you to consciously adopt the appropriate approach related to what you are trying to achieve and the circumstances you face. It is not designed to be prescriptive nor does it suggest that your negotiation should take place at one particular point of the clock face. Many negotiations fluctuate depending on what stage the negotiation is at. The clock face, therefore, is not a process suggesting that you should start at one point and move sequentially to another, it is simply a model which highlights the different styles of negotiation available to us.

The negotiation environment

If we are going to control any negotiation we first have to understand the environment within which we operate. For example, imagine you are responsible for managing a particular customer on an ongoing basis. You feel that a relationship is going to serve your long-term interests, which requires you to build some level of trust and an understanding with your customer. However, your customer has significant market power and exerts pressure on you to improve your terms. This makes your relationship difficult and transactional in nature as their behavior suggests their interests are in short-term gains only.

Do you choose to spend your time at 4 o'clock hard bargaining and risk suboptimizing longer-term opportunities (ignoring other possible variables), or do you attempt to move them around to 10 o'clock to work on the relationship in an attempt to gain a more mutually beneficial solution?

The answer to this again is "it depends." So by understanding the different factors that can influence your negotiations, you can build a stronger awareness of whether you need to proactively change the nature of your relationship with the other party and/or the climate of your meetings during your negotiations.

Bartering: 1 o'clock

Bartering involves the art of trading one thing off against another and does not necessarily involve money. Trade bartering has taken place around the world for thousands of years before money even existed. Today there are websites dedicated to bartering or "swapping."

Price bartering, as anyone who has ever bought that carpet at the Egyptian market stall will know, can be very quick and the final price agreed can be far removed from the market value. Our satisfaction is from having secured the carpet for only $XX when back home it would have cost $YY, regardless of the implications of getting it home or even whether we needed one at all. Both the culture and rituals employed in the Middle East make this form of negotiation process "normal" and comfortable for locals. There is a ritual, a process to go through where we establish the value of something between us. Indeed it is usual for locals to insist on getting to know each other before business can even be discussed. It's common for entire families to be involved in this process. It's how business is done: it involves trust, personality, and, yes, capitalism. It is a process those from the Middle East are far more comfortable with than those conditioned differently in Western cultures.

There need not be any relationship, trust, or even respect, simply a ritual to agree on the price. When bartering, the parties try to pretend that there is respect or trust in what each other is saying. At least when we move around to 3 and 4 o'clock there may not be much trust but there is enough integrity in place that the pretending has stopped. However, when it comes down to conducting business, this is the rawest form of capitalism: how much you want something and how much I need to trade something within our own micro-economy. Nothing else matters. In negotiation terms it's raw, basic, and yet effective. It's at 1 o'clock because it represents about as basic a form of negotiation as you can get. Until money was invented it was the only way to negotiate of material value.

Haggling/bidding: 2–3 o'clock
Websites such as eBay have helped create new industries in the way products and services are traded around the world. The days of the sleepy antique auctions, although still in operation, have been taken over by a vast online bidding industry. Today you can trade almost anything online via designated business auction traders or business-to-consumer (B2C) sites. Even the stock market operates using the process of bidding where

ultimately the market (supply and demand) will define the value of the transaction.

This basic means of agreeing a price demands the greatest of all self-disciplines: being prepared to walk away. The risks of becoming too competitive with no alternative options before entering into a bidding war are well illustrated by the government sell-off of the 3G mobile phone licenses in the UK during 2000. The mobile phone operators ended up paying many times the value for the privilege of gaining one of the four licenses up for auction. You may have thought that these multi-billion-pound businesses would have used sales projections and profit forecasts to work out the limits beyond which they could not go. The other consideration was that there could only be four winners and these were going to be the players who would be around to compete in the future. The view was held that those without the licences would not be able to compete in the future. So the limits the competing companies were prepared to pay became greater than the commercial reality suggested at the time. The "winners" ended up paying £22.5 billion in what became the biggest auction of its kind in modern business. It took a further 8 years before 3G technology took hold of the market and financial returns could start to be realized.

tendering processes
An invitation to tender for the contract by submitting your best proposal against a briefing document.
The organizers will then use this to either form a shortlist or award the contract.

Businesses that use **tendering processes** are effectively using the bidding process to attract a price-based best offer from a range of potential suppliers. Local government contracts widely use this process for subcontracting purposes as part of the procurement process, to ensure that competitive pressures are maintained and that taxpayers are getting "good value." However, where the nature of the contract is based on a performance-related service, for example, the building of a road, price alone, even against a well-specified brief, can prove a restrictive means of agreeing all terms and can lead to poor "total value" agreements. However, without such transparent competitive procedures, government procurement would be more susceptible to illegal forms of bribery.

Many businesses use this 2–3 o'clock approach and build in a post-tender negotiation process with those who have effectively qualified to the final stage of potential suppliers. This allows the negotiation to move around the clock face to a win–win situation at 8 o'clock or beyond, providing for greater synergies to be realized.

Hard bargaining: 4 o'clock

Hard bargaining in its purest form is not typically the preferred approach in B2B negotiations, but even complex negotiations such as those that involve the acquisition of companies frequently move to 4 o'clock on the final issues. This is typically when all the remaining issues have been exhausted and one final issue remains unresolved. It is under these pressured conditions when the skill, mindset, and confidence to hard bargain are both necessary and critical.

"What I get, you lose, and what you get, I lose"

For those who believe in fairness, hard bargaining provides the greatest of tests. It is not fair, it is uncomfortable: it requires nerve and it will make you question whether the discomfort was worth the benefit that came from it. Your opening position is likely to be rejected (if not it would have been inappropriate) and you are likely to be facing someone who is trying to understand how far you will go.

Of course, hard bargaining for yourself is a different experience from doing it on behalf of the company you work for. Although it may not be your preferred approach to negotiation, it has to be understood in order to avoid leaving yourself vulnerable. Where people or companies have power, they will use it to their commercial benefit and if you are not equipped to perform under such circumstances you will pay more than you need to.

The two most important disciplines in any negotiation consist of asking questions and making proposals. Information is power and, at 4 o'clock, power will play a part in how the **bargaining range** is divided. This is

bargaining range
Assuming there is a bargaining range, this is the difference between the most you will pay and the least the other party will accept or vice versa.

rarely transparent. If you told the other party what your break point was (your bottom line), would they be prepared to pay a cent more?

The art of hard bargaining is of course to work out what *their* break point is – that is, negotiate from inside their head.

Once you understand their interests, priorities, time pressures, and options, you will be better positioned to gauge how far and hard you can push. One assumes that the other party is responsible for their own interests. They are unlikely to agree to anything they cannot or don't want to agree to. Your questions will provide you with ever more forms of information and, as a result, help make your position more powerful. If you are not asking questions you should be making a proposal. On the other hand, if you are faced with a skilled hard bargainer who has adopted a silent stance and an extreme position of their own, you must be prepared to hold firm, be patient, and reiterate your position.

Figure 2.2 Hard bargaining positioning.

Delivering a proposal

When stating your proposal, you should set out to create an anchor from which the other person feels that they need to reassess their own expectations. It should be extreme and yet realistic. Too extreme and they may just walk away from any further dialogue. Your opening position is simply the start of a process during which you set out to manage their expectations. Everything becomes relative to this position, even your own concessions, in that you know you will have to move if a deal is to be agreed. Yes, they are going to reject it so get used to the word "no." Yes, they will be emotional as they express their shock and surprise. This is to be expected and is all part of the process. However, if you antagonize or insult the other party, for example, by opening at too extreme a position, you risk losing the chance of maintaining a conversation and ultimately completing the deal, even if you have significant power. So the art of hard bargaining is gauging your opening position and then being tough on issues like price, whilst remaining respectful of the people you are negotiating with. This means:

- appropriate positioning;
- holding tough; and
- conceding on fewer occasions and by lesser amounts than the other party.

In the majority of cases, negotiators who make their offer first will come out ahead.

Another characteristic of hard bargaining anchoring consists of stating a position as a fact early in the dialogue. It can be one of the most powerful tactics available to you for gaining psychological power. In situations where there are no clear market value indicators and there is scope for the perception of value to be different from market value, first offers have an incredibly strong anchoring effect. This relative positioning of what I call "playing at home" exerts a strong pull throughout the rest of the negotiation as counter-offers and moves become relative to the opening anchoring position (your home position). If you start playing away you run the risk of trying to move them from their position, which means you are more likely to finish up closer to their position than to yours. Of course, this is much easier to control if you have a level of real transparent power. For example, it's pretty easy to look confident in a game of poker if you have four aces, but less so with two 3s.

Medium- or long-term positioning can be more subtle. It can occur over weeks, months, or even years, perhaps making the same statement in different ways over many interactions. The statement may firm up as the negotiation approaches, or may be delivered again and again, with the negotiation only occurring when the negotiator deems the anchoring positioning to have created the right conditions and timing for success to be more likely.

Dealing: 5–6 o'clock

The timing of the contract (the sooner the contract can be completed) may have as much benefit to me as it has a downside to you: bonus payments may be as costly for you to achieve as they are for me to provide. So although each agenda item needs agreeing and perhaps even trading, they may not necessarily provide any incremental benefit. Where you are faced with simply agreeing on terms, which provide little by way of any real incremental benefit, a deal-like climate is likely to exist and the need to be considered, conditional, and tough during your dealings is critical to you in protecting your position and the value of the deal.

The process of deal-making is usually made up of trade-offs and compromises rather than of low-cost, high-value trades as found in classic win–win situations. This is because, where time pressures are in play and there is a need to make the deal work, trades tend to be made up of "necessary" moves to make the deal work rather than value-adding activity, although the two are not mutually exclusive. Deal-making can involve few issues, which means the style and dialogue can sometimes be little more than hard bargaining, although the climate tends to be more respectful. The difference is that you can offer to move on one issue, providing them with some satisfaction subject to a reciprocal move on another allowing for the deal to be completed. Price, as we know, is the most contentious and transparent of all variables, which is why, when negotiated alone, it tends to lead to competitive forms of negotiation. When dealing is in play at 5–6 o'clock there can be three or four issues involved, each of which are transparent and, although they need agreeing, they provide little by way of opportunity for mutual gain.

Concession trading: 6–7 o'clock

This is the first of the collaborative approaches where both parties recognize that some level of cooperation is required if mutual interests are to progress. The more common interests that can be identified between the two parties, the greater the potential for creating value. The process can involve conditional trade-offs across a broad range of issues from a pre-agreed agenda.

The negotiation climate is usually constructive but still guarded. For example, saying "if you place the order today, we will guarantee you your required time slot," would seem to be an offer to move things around to accommodate the other party. It could, however, be the case that you were going to do this anyway, that there is no cost implication in offering the time slot or that you have very few orders so they could have had any time slot without any implications to you. All that matters is that you were seen to offer a conditional concession (in this case, the condition that the order is placed today) and were providing some value (convenience and security of securing an important time slot), leaving the other party with the satisfaction that they have agreed a *"good deal"* with you.

Now that you are on the left-hand, collaborative side of the clock face, your focus should be on working "on the deal." Nothing is agreed until everything is agreed, which means that you can park issues or variables and come back to them if not agreed on. An unresolved issue does not mean there is a deadlock, but that other issues need to be examined in order to help resolve the current impasse.

Win–win: 8 o'clock

Win–win implies by its very definition that both sides in a negotiation win or come out ahead. The rational process of trading low-cost, high-value issues in such a way that the total value opportunity can be enhanced was popularized in the 1980s in the book *Getting to Yes* by Ury and Fisher. The concept of win–win assumes that both parties will make decisions based on the fact that, if one party offers you something of greater value than that which they seek, in return leaving you with an incremental gain, then you are more likely to accept it. If your aim is to build value, it's difficult to argue with the theory. However, as Ury and Fisher later went on to write in *Beyond Reason*, the emotional side of a relationship plays a significant part in how agreements actually come together. People are not always rational in their behavior.

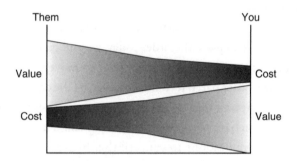

Figure 2.3 Low-cost, high-value win–win trade-offs.

During 2015 Facebook progressed a strategy of building relationships with publishers including the BBC, Bild, NBC news, and *The New York Times*, amongst others. The concept (called *Instant Articles*) attracted nine publishers who committed to provide news information to Facebook. This in turn attracted audiences to their own monetized solutions, of which they were able to keep 100% of those revenues. It was apparent to the publishers that Facebook were in fact competing with Yahoo, Google, and Twitter, securing exclusive social media feeds. The negotiations resulted in the publishers taking control over which stories appeared and ensured that, by embracing social media, their own online business model would not be undermined. The agreement facilitated by Facebook sought to build on the mutual interests of those involved, focus on the longer-term picture, and measure success through the synergy and strengthening this would bring to their own users. The win–win agreement had only been made possible because of the collaborative approach this engendered.

From 8 o'clock onwards you have the option of sharing some information in order to help the other party to help you. This of course requires a higher level of trust than when simply concession trading. Trust takes time to earn and can be more easily nurtured when the balance of power is more even or when the dominant party has a genuine motive for securing your commitment to an agreement.

Partnership joint problem solving: 9–10 o'clock

When building an agenda for a 9–10 o'clock negotiation, your mindset should be focused on forming a sustainable agreement that covers all areas, including:

- performance;
- compliance; and
- risk.

Take the concept of total value agreements that are central to win–win negotiations and extend the possibilities through building more dependency between parties. For instance, if this benefits us, it will benefit you; if it harms us, it will harm you. Focus your attention on what issues could create problems during the lifetime of the agreement for both parties. Take your time working through the level of risk and responsibilities that both of you are prepared to take. Then build an agreement ensuring that responsibility is transparent and clearly stated and that risk is clearly compensated for.

Relationship building: 11–12 o'clock

The value of partnership in business cannot be underestimated. It often represents the optimum position for building agreements – when trading partners are interdependent and there is a clear need to help each other to realize the efficiencies, synergies, and saving as part of how they work continuously together. It is an "ideal" situation and in some cases works but very often proves difficult to achieve and sustain. Why? Performance change and changes in the market result in an ever-shifting environment. Sometimes these changes have been factored into the agreement and sometimes they serve to expose one party or the other. At 10–12 o'clock, risks will have been considered as part of the original agreement. However, if one party suffers as a result of change that could result in the trading relationship being affected, both parties are more likely to reappraise the trading arrangement and sometimes even renegotiate the terms. The degree of interdependency in play means both parties are implicated if one is affected by change.

When negotiating past 10 o'clock your agenda should be designed to encourage transparency, creativity, and possibility. In essence, the broader the agenda the greater the scope for building robust deals with added value. Examining longevity, intangibles (things that are not material), risk, sustainability, information, resources, and so on allows for highly creative agreements to be built that reflect all of the interests, needs for flexibility, and potential opportunities for both parties. However, this ideal requires understanding and patience and in some cases an acceptance that the reduced risks achieved by longer-term agreements may have to come at the cost of short-term margin or profit maximization. If that is desirable then the partnership approach may well prove appropriate. Much will depend on the circumstances and objectives of those involved.

Back to bartering (1 o'clock)

In his book *The Undercover Economist*, Tim Harford explains how the cost and value of a cup of coffee can vary and why the average commuter is prepared to pay a premium for a cup of coffee at the train station or airport when time is a premium and supply and demand are in favor of the well-positioned coffee kiosk. Although you may be a regular customer of the kiosk as you rush to the office, and may have become loyal to a particular brand of coffee as a result, your relationship is not a partnership. Indeed, the balance of power as a result of supply and demand is still firmly in favor of the strategically positioned coffee kiosk. Your ability and your motive to negotiate in public over a few cents is removed. Also, the kiosks with loyalty scheme cards effectively constitute a proposal made to their loyal customers: a retrospective discount, a loyalty incentive, more coffee rather than a lower price, a trade barter, and low-cost, high-value incentive, which takes us past 12 o'clock and back to what we started with: bartering.

Exploring the reality of partnerships

Partnerships provide the necessary veneer enabling many agreements to be progressed in business. Some corporations believe so strongly in partnerships that their values and ethics heavily promote them through and across their business.

Ethical partnerships carry a sense of righteousness about them. Few companies would openly admit that they are out to screw every last cent out of their customers or suppliers and yet they are required to provide statements about maximizing shareholder value. Again this cannot always be achieved without someone else paying and, the larger the organization, the more leverage they have for doing so. I am not suggesting that partnerships do not exist, but in all my experience in business they are rarely as idealistic or as reflective as the true definition of partnership might suggest. Formed partnerships take the form of unions, marriages, cooperatives, societies, confederations, alliances, associations, and institutions, and there are many more entities based on common interests, values, and motives for investment. By their very nature, two or more businesses working together are going to be challenged – they will have independent interests to consider and you must always remain mindful and aware of these considerations.

Where partnerships work effectively is where the relationship is of *strategic* importance, that is, where the businesses could easily be compromised if the relationship were not to "perform" and that the investment in time and effort delivers obvious mutual synergy benefits. Although partnerships perform better with trust, trust can take time to earn and requires the glue of dependency. Once it exists it can also be harmful in that it can serve to disarm, promoting familiarity and complacency. So a continued balancing act needs to be "policed" through measurement and performance reviews for the partnership to be sustainable. These considerations should feature early in the negotiation agenda as being critical to the sustainability of any agreement that you may build.

KEY TAKEAWAYS

There are no right or wrong ways to negotiate, and no fixed way of ensuring that you will always get the best agreement. The clock face helps to differentiate and recognize those behaviors and strategies in play and what these are likely to do to value, rather than simply suggesting a right way of negotiating, which would be highly exposing.

- The clock face simply serves as a compass to help you adopt the appropriate approach for each of your negotiations.
- Many negotiations will move around the clock during the negotiation, so never assume a constant.
- Your approach and behavior can help you to move the other party around the clock face to suit your preferred strategy.
- It's easier to build and grow value cooperatively and collaboratively between 8 and 12 o'clock.
- The right-hand side of the clock face typically represents more competitive and transactional negotiations.
- Where the balance of power is strongly in favor of one party, the tendency is for the negotiation to take place or end up in the 1–6 o'clock environment.

CHAPTER 3

Why Power Matters

"You only have power over people so long as you don't take every-thing away from them. When you've robbed a man of everything, he's no longer in your power – he's free again."

Aleksandr Solzhenitsyn

WHAT DO WE MEAN BY POWER?

You are as powerful as others perceive you to be, which is limiting if you do not understand how they see the situation. Power can be real or perceived, or as subjective as it is objective in that it exists in people's heads; even though the other party may be dependent on you or independent of you. Power can shift, can be created from time and circumstance, and can be used to nurture or exploit. So clearly it needs to be understood and respected.

Why the balance of power matters

So why is power so important in negotiations? Quite simply, it provides you with options and, if understood, will enable you to control where on the clock face your negotiation will take place.

- **Holding the balance of power.** If you hold the balance of power in your relationship(s), you have greater scope to control the agenda, the process, and ultimately influence the negotiation in your favor.

- **Power to influence the climate, style, strategy, and possibilities.** Power provides you with the opportunity to choose between being competitive or collaborative, depending on which suits your purpose and objectives.

Creating the perception of power *before* the negotiation begins can be achieved through demonstrating indifference, outlining your options, or the other party's lack of options. All are designed to manage expectations and suggest that you are negotiating from a position of strength. Trying to do so once discussions have begun is transparent and can prove futile. The Complete Skilled Negotiator understands the value of clearly framing the facts surrounding the circumstances of those involved so as to enhance their perceived power.

Holding the balance of power

History has taught us that those with power will at some point seek to exercise it. Therefore, it is vital to understand the balance of power, be clear where the negotiation is likely to take place on the clock face, and prepare accordingly. The type of relationship you have with those you negotiate with will directly influence how and where you choose to negotiate on the clock face.

One of the most important considerations when gauging power will be the amount of *information* available relating to each party's circumstances. The degree to which time and circumstances are transparent directly affects the power balance within your relationship and the style of negotiation that is most likely to follow. That is not to suggest that those who enter a negotiation from a weak position enter as lambs ready for the slaughter: very often the more powerful party will use the situation to gain other forms of value such as loyalty, exclusivity, or greater flexibility, rather than just beating the other party into agreeing a lower price. Where you negotiate on the clock face will impact on all these possibilities and on the total value opportunity that will be created from your discussions. So we need to treat power respectfully if we are to make the most of it. The purpose of this is not so that you can win or beat the other party. They are not your competition. It is to help you optimize value from the negotiations you are preparing for.

HOW DOES POWER INFLUENCE NEGOTIATIONS?

Influencing factors

Those factors which have the greatest influence on where negotiations take place on the clock face are made up of the following:

1. The level of dependency.
2. The power of the brand and the relative size of both parties.
3. History/precedents.
4. Competitor activity and changing market conditions.
5. The party with more time.
6. The nature of the product, service, or contract.
7. Personal relationships.

1. The level of dependency

Who needs who the most, or the level of dependency between both parties, directly influences the balance of power between you and those you negotiate with. If you don't need to do a deal and are not dependent on the other party, your position of "indifference" provides you with a greater level of power, assuming that you both know this and believe it to be true. Any need to form an agreement is usually influenced by your circumstances, whatever they may be.

In economic terms this is referred to as supply and demand.

- If there is an abundance of supply and little demand, the buyers, assuming they have a need, will have more power available to them.
- If the product or service is in short supply yet demand is high, the seller will more likely have greater power.

Quite simply, if there is a shortage or difficulty in acquiring something, assuming that demand is stable or strong, then the value will increase. In times of no demand or when there is oversupply the value or price will generally drop. Although this is the case in most market situations it is not always so apparent. Asking the right questions will help you to clarify this.

- How is your supplier performing generally, and how important does this make you to them?
- How many options, other than you, do they have to achieve their strategic objectives?
- If demand for the product has slowed, how much more important has this made your agreement?

The more demand you are able to create, the more options you have, and the more powerful your position will be in just about any type of negotiation.

Although not always possible, one of the most effective ways of building power for yourself is by developing BATNAs (Best Alternative to a Negotiated Agreement), because the more options you have, the stronger you become.

The clearer your options, the more definitive your own break point will be.

Understanding and building options or BATNAs is fundamental to establishing power. **No options = no power**, or at least from inside your own head.

The supply of money on the money markets influences the best mortgage rates available for home buying. These rates are regularly published in the press as banks compete to lend money against the security of property. Some take the time to talk to a mortgage broker who will provide a range of options based on their circumstances; some will approach the bank or mortgage company who will outline their latest offer, or they may simply be advised of the cost of extending their current mortgage without providing any other options. However, those who genuinely shop around, research on the internet, and talk with a number of suppliers effectively get a feel for what the best on the market is. Along with a BATNA, knowing that you can go elsewhere ensures that the time invested in research pays off. The best deals are not necessarily the ones advertised. In the world of private banking there are many deals available for the right person at below high-street prices, subject to the right relationship and broader circumstances. With a high-street BATNA to hand it's worth progressing such discussions.

Qualifying the other party's options, and therefore their power, requires us to question objectively the viability of the options they say they have. In some industries there are substantial costs in implementing an option. For instance, the set-up costs of switching manufacturers may be considerable: re-tooling, resourcing materials, new safety inspections; not to mention the disruption, ongoing training, and relationship building that needs to take place. The other party may be able to employ their BATNA, but they may be unwilling to actually implement it.

So creating power where you can control supply and demand can be a highly effective way of strengthening your negotiation position. It is important, then, to understand power and how it impacts on your expectations and those of the other party. The way most people gauge power is from instinctive, subjective insights formed from observations of the other party, or more often on clear factual market evidence. If you are the only supplier who can deliver what your customer cannot do without, they are likely to pay as much as they need to get what they want.

For example, the oil industry has for many years controlled its output in terms of how many millions of barrels of oil are produced in any given week. This has a direct impact on the price of petrol at the pumps.

Where the balance of power is strongly in favor of one party and the need for cooperation during the negotiation is not necessary, that party can drive very tough negotiations. **Dependency imbalance** can result in the negotiation swinging around to the right-hand (competitive) side of the clock face.

In a business-to-business (B2B) context, absolute dependency leads to absolute power, which can promote corruption and make for poor business. This is why governments have competition and monopolies acts to manage extreme cases of non-competitive market manipulation. Creating options or a best alternative before entering your negotiation is an effective way of reducing dependency and, in doing so, reduces the power of the other party. Creating a BATNA is therefore an important element of preparation (see Chapter 9). For as long as you have total dependency on one supplier or buyer, and assuming that they know this, you will be negotiating from a position of weakness.

dependency imbalance
Where one party has a greater dependency on the other (real or perceived), resulting in them having less negotiating power.

Of course, few relationships are so one-sided or remain so for very long. Power is often measured in a subjective manner, meaning that feelings, instinct, circumstance, and behavior also contribute to the way you weigh up any given situation.

On the many occasions I have facilitated negotiation planning sessions across teams with various clients, I ask the question about power: "Who has the balance of power in your business relationship, you or the buyer/seller?" On over 70% of occasions, the initial response is: "the other party!" Why? Because most of us live inside our own head. We find it difficult to see, feel, or understand the pressures that the other party is experiencing, so we focus on those to which we are exposed and this of course undermines our own position of power. Negotiating from inside your own head is a very dangerous place to be. The balance of power between those involved in the majority of negotiations is much closer than most will allow themselves to believe.

As a Complete Skilled Negotiator it is important to recognize that, even where the market power is clearly stacked against you, you can set out to change the dependencies between you and shift the balance of power.

CREATING OPTIONS

Launching a new product onto the market takes a lot of careful planning. Agreeing terms and commitments comes pretty high on the list and the way your plans are communicated can significantly change the attitude of others. Who needs who the most here? Your options could be who you offer what levels of investment to. Who you offer exclusivity, marketing, extended ranges, or protections of terms based on volumes to. You may even enjoy market power where you have several suppliers or customer options so can create competitive tension. Whatever the environment, you need options or best alternatives.

One challenge for account managers who manage only one customer is that the customer is aware of this and knows just how important they are to the account manager sat in front of them. You may even be part of a team dedicated to managing the one account and the buyer knows this only too well.

So who has the balance of power in this situation? How do you calculate power and does it really matter? As always, it depends. However, what I have found is that in a majority of cases the balance of power is not as fixed or as one-sided as most are prepared to believe.

Even where you can't choose your customers, you can choose which ones to invest in, which ones to partner with, which ones to work more proactively with, to strategically differentiate and then ensure they understand that your business has options to offer this elsewhere.

Whether you sell insurance, energy, engineering parts, consultancy services, or tins of tomatoes the same dynamics apply.

Make the time to be proactive, plan out your options, and, where appropriate, make them known. Make the time to create alternatives and you will be able to manage the balance of power more effectively.

2. The power of the brand and the relative size of both parties

Imagine you are responsible for selling an established mega-branded soft drink. You know that any retailer will sell more of your brand than their own brand or a lesser branded soft drink. The retailer accepts that margins will be lower due to the high investment in the brand itself, but this is offset by being able to sell higher quantities.

The retailer will probably sell their cheaper, higher-margin own brand as well, resulting in their overall product and margin mix being optimized.

Significant amounts of money are invested in building brands. As part of establishing the brands some manufacturers have even, for limited periods, supplied products to the distributors or retailers at no margin at all, or even at below cost. The aim here is to expose their product to the market as part of creating demand, brand awareness, and attracting market share. In the long term, brand power and the terms that can be negotiated with a strong brand will more than outweigh the market entry costs.

In some cases, retail buyers need to stock certain lines in order to make their product category credible to their customers and also to remain competitive with other retailers. In doing so, they will list branded products despite having to operate at lower margins. So both extremes are in play here: brands are built and represent power within a negotiation in that the buyer needs them, but the same brands with which account managers need exposure to maintain their market share position can carry limited power. Who needs whom the most and why? What brands bring to the broader business case in terms of their reliability, quality, and customer loyalty will have some bearing on the considerations of the buyer, as they seek to optimize their profitability, starting by objectively weighing up the balance of power within the relationship.

USING BRAND POWER

A European health and beauty retail chain listed more than 10,000 lines in its stores. With their broad proposition they stocked baby wipes at one end of the spectrum and top-branded fragrances at the other.

Their team of buyers dealt with over 250 suppliers and agents with a range of relationships that directly impacted on the way negotiations were conducted.

The hair coloring category represented 5% of their total sales, yet attracted 31% of the total market for Europe. Their own hair coloring was cheap, reliable, and accessible to the price conscious. The volumes were significant. The negotiations with their main own-brand supplier were margin focused and tough. The buyers knew that the supplier had a high level of dependency on the trading relationship and would use this power to their own ends.

The negotiations with the "super-brands" had more obvious options for the supplier due to its own "brand product power." The negotiations were collaborative and included trade-offs such as exclusive packaging and pack sizes, joint advertising, and buy back where the supplier offered to uplift at cost overstocks from previous promotional activities. The supplier regarded this as a worthwhile investment whilst the retailer regarded it as a "problem solved." They both regarded negotiations as joint business planning aimed at growing their total category. For the buyers their interest was the average category margin – getting the balance between high margin own brand sales and high volume branded sales making the best use of the credibility afforded from the presence of the super-brands in their stores.

Although most B2B negotiations benefit from collaboration, creativity and a focus on total value opportunities, the reality is that there are many relationships that work because of dependency.

anchoring position
A position which is designed to anchor the expectations and movement of the other party.

3. History/precedents

History and precedents also play a part in influencing how people seek to rationalize and legitimize their position: "Last time we agreed to a discount of 15% on volumes in excess of $3 million so let's start at 15%." Current terms can serve as the rationale for an **anchoring position.**

Previous positions, all else remaining equal, serve to shape expectations. Many organizations work hard to address this through the continuous innovation of products or changing the nature of the service they offer: they seek to remove the "apples for apples" comparisons. To achieve this, many may decide to:

- change the people responsible for the relationship;
- move historical understandings; or
- change the package, service offer, or product being supplied.

It is quite normal for organizations to do this as part of ensuring that trading remains competitive.

Often where change takes place, when a new person or team is assigned an account, or where a recent acquisition of a competitor takes place and new personalities come into play, objectives and motives of the new players can change quickly, bringing with them a move away from how the business will have been conducted in the past. Many organizations systematically move their buyers around so as to ensure that historical dealings can be ignored more easily.

In other cases, such as in corporate banking, great value is placed on established relationships and mutual experience that have taken years to build, and the value that these relationships offer can add to the collaborative way that the relationship is managed. In each case there is the knowledge of how business has been conducted in the past, which is used to influence how it should be in the future.

4. Competitor activity and market conditions

During the credit crunch in 2007/8, a period of unprecedented uncertainty was experienced by most industries in the US and across Europe.

Commercial property prices, business values, future earnings forecasts, and ultimately earnings multiples were all severely hit. Companies with high levels of debt became more vulnerable and even companies with strong forward order books looked less secure. Market assumptions relating to risks were challenged; cash became king as commodity prices hit record highs along with the cost of oil and the radical shift in behavior of the banking industry. Literally within months, long-term commitments were difficult to attract as risk aversion became critical to survival. These changes had tested just about every forecast assumption, resulting in many contracts being negotiated or renegotiated in an entirely different climate and style to that of the original agreement.

The unpredictability of change affects the degree to which people are prepared to commit and the level of risk they are prepared to accommodate. In other words, stability and certainty promote a basis for longer-term commitments. In our ever-changing and fast-paced world, the issue of change plays an important part in any negotiation, in terms of what is being discussed, the length of any agreement and which party is more exposed to the influence of uncontrollable change.

Although change affects risk and value it can also affect power. Your competitors' innovation, marketing, and strategy will have some bearing on what your customers regard as their options. The very fact that your competitors are competing provides more power to your customers during negotiations. For example, in electronics the exclusive launch of a new high-end, 80-inch, 3D, HD plasma TV that attracts 10% of the retail sales in its target market will directly affect the sales of its competitors' TVs. This in turn will influence their trading performance and the power they have with their retail and wholesale customers.

5. The party with more time

Time and circumstances offer the greatest of power levers in negotiation. If you have been effective at getting inside the other party's head and understand their time pressures, you will have more power to exert. How you choose to use this will depend on your objectives, the depenancy within your relationship and the overall shape of the deal.

Any company operating under pressure, whether it is to make a decision, place an offer or conclude a deal, is compromised by time pressure and will already be placing a premium on doing whatever is necessary to meet their deadline. Your job as a negotiator is to test and qualify the priorities and interests of the other party all the time, as the value or perceived value of just about anything is constantly changing. A party who is prepared to pay more today as a result of time pressures may not be in the same position next week. So if you leave the opportunity too long you may lose the power you had as their circumstances change.

But what if the timing of a deal is not naturally in your favor? The other party could have many options and can reject your ideas and proposals. The answer is to orchestrate events in such a way that you build power by taking control of time and circumstance. But how can this be possible?

If time and circumstances affect options, then, by creating circumstances through the sequencing of events, you can effectively take control and negotiate from a greater position of power.

TAKING CONTROL OF TIME AND CIRCUMSTANCES

Sequencing events by mapping your negotiation process can be used to create momentum and power. Sequencing allows you to proactively manage events and communication aimed at helping you remain in control of the overall process.

One notable example of this was where the legal team of a US private equity firm managed to sequence the events surrounding a business purchase, based on the pending and predictable change in exchange rates.

During 2015 the euro exchange rate experienced significant fluctuations against the dollar as a result of the real threat of Greece defaulting on debt and the introduction of quantitative easing in mainland Europe. Meanwhile deflation was looming and general consumer spending was flat. A discount grocery retailer backed by the US private equity firm was continuing to expand its operations. Negotiations had been ongoing for 12 months over the acquisition of a further small chain of established stores (Priceline) with prime positions in Belgium.

The economic trend was no secret nor was the trading performance of Priceline. The PE firm recognized, however, that if they sequenced the conclusion of their timing discussions with the first release of quantitative easing in Europe, this would trigger a jump in the value of the dollar and the deal could be closed with a 3% reduction in cost in dollars. They made a time limited improvement on their offer of 2% for two weeks. Circumstances had allowed them to impose a legitimate time limited offer against the currency risk, which the board of Priceline recognized and ultimately agreed to.

6. The nature of the product, service, or contract

Negotiating a complex construction deal or business merger is, by its very nature, more challenging than buying a car from your local garage. Alternatively, agreeing a contract for IT services, by its very nature, requires a different type of process and agenda than, say, agreeing a settlement following a marriage breakdown. The different relationships in play and the nature of the outcomes required result in most negotiations being unique.

Example: buying a car

If you were buying a second-hand car privately, you would probably set about agreeing a price with the current owner. Two pieces of information would help set the parameters for discussion. First, the price that the owner is asking, which is effectively their opening position, and, second, what the model and age of car would typically sell for in the market. Both parties will be aware of this and usually end up negotiating around the price. The buyer may seek to lower the seller's aspirations by pointing to some work that the car needs doing to bring it up to scratch. The seller may try to increase its perceived value by promoting the reliability of the car and the fact that it has only had one owner. Neither argument need make any difference to the negotiation unless you choose to listen to them. There is no prospect of a relationship following the deal, few issues to negotiate around, so a hard bargaining or deal making negotiation is likely to follow (4–5 o'clock on the clock face).

Now imagine you were in a position to spend more money and decided to purchase from a local dealer. Can the worn tire be replaced? Will they tax the car? Can they provide competitive finance arrangements? Both the possibility of a relationship beyond the immediate agreement and a broader agenda to discuss could result in the negotiation being more appropriately conducted in a concession trading or even a win–win environment (7–8 o'clock on the clock face).

Finally, consider the same transaction, but this time you are considering buying a new car from a main dealer. Servicing, depreciation and future trade-in guarantees, extras on the car, and even insurance now start to feature in your discussions. Total value becomes a greater consideration and the deal may well take place in a joint problem solving or even a relationship building environment (10–11 o'clock on the clock face).

What has changed over these three scenarios is the breadth of issues which can be discussed and the possibility of a relationship that goes beyond that of the transaction. The item, a car, remains broadly the same but in each case the appropriate style of negotiation changes.

There is no right or wrong. Your responsibility as a negotiator is to weigh up what you are trying to achieve and decide which process is more likely to cover the broad range of risks and benefits involved.

7. Personal relationships

In every culture, relationships and trust play a part in the climate of negotiations. Building an understanding of each other's position and needs through exploratory meetings is critical if broader agendas other than price are to be entertained. Most people prefer doing business with people they trust and respect. The degree to which trust exists will almost always influence the climate of openness and the position on the clock face where the negotiation takes place.

Respect has to be earned and is more likely to be achieved through being consistent and reliable rather than by being over-flexible or agreeing to make unconditional concessions. In my experience, even if you feel others are being unfair, inconsiderate, unyielding, or even arrogant in their dealings, you need to look beyond behavior and make a rational, sober, unemotional assessment of the balance of power. Emotional responses to the positions and demands of the other party will only play to their advantage. Similarly, if you are in a position of strength, use it to assert your position and gain commitments, but not to aggravate the situation. Remember that negotiation is not about "winning" in the sense of beating the other party.

Without some degree of trust your negotiations are likely at best to feel transactional and difficult. Equally, with too much familiarity, complacency kicks in and the total value, opportunity, becomes compromised. The challenge for you is to find the right balance to serve your interests.

INFORMATION IS POWER

If you could read the minds of the other party you would be able to see the options available, understand their true cost base, their time pressures, the real implications of having no agreement, and so on. Unfortunately, such transparency rarely exists. However, you can still unearth some of this information by questioning, exploring, and listening to various stakeholders in order to understand the circumstances of the other party.

Information about the other person's options or circumstances certainly provides power, so for the same reasons you should seriously consider how much information and what type of information is appropriate for you to share with them. Building power requires you to think and operate like a barrister, but not an interrogator, questioning appropriately to gain insights. Approach the issues from different angles. This is not about interrogating, as we have

(Continued)

(*Continued*)

to manage the relationships involved. It is about understanding the whole situation; using your curiosity, inquisitiveness, and desire to clarify the issues as they see them. The more you invest in understanding their motives, dives, and objectives, the more powerful your position becomes.

It is for this reason that questioning and listening are critical behaviors of negotiators. Negotiating in a vacuum (not understanding the market around you) can only result in you operating inside your own head and therefore suboptimizing your opportunities.

Quite simply, information is power.

IT'S WORTH WHATEVER THEY WILL AGREE TO

Supply and demand is one of the more straightforward economic levers used universally through the stock exchange, auction houses, the cost of an airline flight, or today's bitcoin value. These are all driven by demand and how much the other party is prepared to pay. Of course, when negotiating, this can only be helpful if you understand the circumstances of the other party: their options or best alternative, their means to pay, and their specific circumstances. Without this understanding, you risk guessing and negotiating from a blinkered position. If you have no understanding of the level of demand, you have little power to work with, even where there is a real demand.

Between June 2011 and March 2015 the Liv-ex Bordeaux fine wine index had dropped from 360 to 240 in value and private collectors struggled to offload their "investments." John Sturgess had fallen on tough times. His business was struggling and he was just managing to meet his monthly outgoings. His wife was about to turn

60 and he wanted to treat her to a holiday, but had conceded that this would only be possible by borrowing. The one asset John had with value was his wine cellar, which he had built up over the years. The value of the French first growths had put him off drinking them. "You just don't drink a £2,000 bottle of wine with your BBQ," he would say.

John decided to make use of the 120 bottles of various chateaux and sell them to fund the holiday. He had never considered disposing of them before so researched on the internet. Auction houses, private buyers, and specialty wine purchasing companies were all offering their services. The auction house would take weeks, then there were fees to consider and of course the uncertainty of what they might fetch (although by now he had worked out what he thought was the market value). Private buyers all seemed to be at the other end of the country. John felt that if they were prepared to travel this far, they might try to barter him down.

Eventually, John decided to call a specialist business and invited them to his house to value his wine. Two well-spoken young connoisseurs arrived the next morning and immediately struck up a conversation with John about how he had come across the wines, where they had been stored, and why he was selling such fine wines at a time when the market was falling in value. John was very open with then, explaining about the holiday, that he probably would not drink them and how he would be pleased to see the back of them at the right price.

The two young men were left in the cellar for 2 hours before reappearing. "The problem we have," they started, "is that as good as the wines are, they have no provenance. They have been stored in your cellar so their value in the market is 50% less than if they had been in a bonded warehouse."

"OK," said John, "so what's the value?"

(Continued)

(*Continued*)

"Well, as you probably know, the market has been dropping for 2 years and although your Latour 96 cases will hold quite well, you have other wines which are close to their drink by date."

"OK, so how much?" said John.

"When do you need payment by?"

John repeated, "Well, as I told you, by the end of the week would be ideal."

The two young men looked at each other. Well versed in this charade, they presented a written list that they had created in the cellar. "We can arrange for a bank transfer here and now, although we know this value will be short of what you were looking for." John's reaction was a natural one: shock. The offer of £60,000 was half what he was expecting. "We'll let you think on it," said one of them. John considered the prospects of the money being immediately available, and not having to go through this process again with others and – you guessed it – he took the deal. The two young connoisseurs had understood John's circumstances, were looking to optimize their margins selling back into the market and had other enquiries to move on to. John may well have attracted more at the auction but would have missed his wife's 60th, which he had allowed to serve as a key criteria.

THE POWER OF A THREE-TIERED STRATEGY

A frozen food logistics firm had successfully built a customer base across Australian grocers based on reliability and best-in-class information tracking. They were about to enter some challenging negotiations with the well-versed retailers. They planned to introduce an average 4% cost increase. They had 12 customers – two of which were by far the largest, making up 50% of total market share.

They categorized each customer by size and location. They further analyzed where conditions existed that would allow them to secure early wins (agreements) and were more likely to attract a commitment without serious implications. These smaller grocers were positioned in phase one of discussions, which took only 2 weeks to complete. As negotiations were concluded, the agreements were "celebrated" via press announcements.

At the time, phase two was commencing with some of the more challenging negotiations which included the "discount retailers." Some precedents were in place (early agreements from phase one), which implied that the terms were being accepted in the market. The toughest category of customers – the two key customers that made up 50% market share – was saved till phase three. Since 50% had already been agreed, this provided power to the logistics firm. They were now in a more powerful position by virtue of market precedents being set. If necessary, they could also introduce tiered time slots favoring their phase one and two customers, if the phase three customers were not prepared to agree. The phasing of the negotiations had created power against the odds and momentum, which helped make agreements across all customers possible.

TACTICAL PLAY

Tactics can be used as a way of delivering implied threats or consequences used to manipulate a situation. This is sometimes done through introducing false time lines or ultimatums which have been imposed by a higher authority such as the other party's boss. These are used when trying to apply pressure or to create urgency. If the other party attempts to apply these, qualify them. Ask them what will happen

(Continued)

> (*Continued*)
>
> next without asking the types of leading questions that could result in you digging a hole for yourself such as "so you have no movement on this issue then?" The idea behind qualifying such claims is to try and establish if gamesmanship is in play. Of course they are never going to admit to this, so it is your role to gauge the likelihood of risk, given all the information you can gather.
>
> Although transparency helps to wipe away some of the "mist" when deciding the difference between real and implied threats, you need to gain as much clarity as possible. Without clarity, you will be operating from an unclear if not compromised position, regardless of what the balance of power might suggest.

If power is directly affected by circumstance then supply and demand represents one of the main issues that influence it. If there is a shortage or difficulty in acquiring something, assuming that demand is stable or strong, then the market value will increase. That does not mean that it has to increase for you. That depends on the situation. In times of no demand or when there is oversupply, the value or price will generally drop. Again, the market rule need not always apply. It depends.

KEY TAKEAWAYS

Power influences strategies and tactics employed, provides one party over another with more options and therefore advantages, yet should not be assumed. With the right strategy, those with the power stacked against them can still negotiate very good deals.

- The balance of power is not a constant and can easily move as time and circumstances or supply and demand dynamics change.
- Proactive positioning can help you create enough power to defend your position.

- Real and perceived power can be equally effective in gaining advantage.
- The common laws of capitalism do not always apply. It really does depend on whose head you are in.
- The stronger your options, the more powerful you become.
- If they have power, expect them to use it.

CHAPTER 4

The Ten Negotiation Traits

"Until you make the unconscious, conscious, it will direct your life and you will call it fate."

C.G. Jung

Self-awareness comes from knowing and being honest with yourself about who you are, what you do, and how you perform.

Most people like to regard themselves as good negotiators. Yet when asked why they think they perform well, they can usually only describe a few of their strengths, or things they believe make a difference to their performance. If the clock face has taught us anything, it has demonstrated that different types of negotiation require different skills. In other words, hard bargaining at 4 o'clock on the clock face requires strengths that are different from those required to perform effectively when joint problem solving at 10 o'clock. However, before moving on to examine how to adapt your behavior as you move around the clock face it is worth understanding how personal traits can influence your overall ability when trying to secure the best deal. To a sports professional, examples of relevant traits might be stamina, agility, speed, and flexibility. These will be important to different degrees, depending on the sport they specialize in. They help to define a player's potential and those areas that require further development as part of improving their overall performance. Some traits are innate and some can be learned or improved on. Importantly, these traits underpin the player's ability to behave and perform to the highest levels in competitive environments.

The ten traits

---

1. Nerve

2. Self-discipline

3. Tenacity

4. Assertiveness

5. Instinct

6. Caution

7. Curiosity

8. Numerical reasoning

9. Creativity

10. Humility

These traits directly influence the actions you take and can be developed through a more conscious approach to how you negotiate. They relate to those attributes that come more naturally to you or those you are more likely to gravitate towards. What is important here is that you think about how these traits influence you and your performance when you negotiate. The ten traits underpin your behavior. For example, maintaining your nerve supports your ability to think clearly when faced with conflict and to open a negotiation with an extreme and yet realistic position. If you handle pressure well and have the nerve to maintain self-control comfortably, your performance in tougher negotiations where competitive behaviors are required will come more naturally. Your traits are neither good nor bad; they are just a reflection of who you are. The important point is to understand yourself well enough to compensate for that which does *not* come naturally and of course to use your strengths to your advantage.

1. NERVE

Believe in your position, never offend, and always remain calm
Nerve helps us to exercise patience and to remain calm when the pressure is on. Anyone operating under pressure is reliant on controlling their nerves as part of being able to perform. The pilot, golfer, police officer,

barrister, to name but a few, rely on their nerve to be able to carry out their duties, as will you when you negotiate.

Exercising nerve during negotiations involves handling both perceived and real conflict, being able to read the sensitivities around the situation before responding. Nothing happens by accident in negotiation, so having a clear head that allows you to operate as a **conscious negotiator** is essential to staying in control. Nerve also enables you to introduce challenging opening positions where appropriate in the knowledge that you are taking a risk that could compromise the potential of a deal. It allows you to more easily demonstrate conviction when taking up a position with confidence.

the conscious negotiator
In negotiation, nothing happens by accident. The conscious negotiator is aware of everything which happens in the room and their every action, comment or interaction is intentional and considered.

Opening with an extreme position and remaining silent where appropriate might be described in some contexts as aggressive or even arrogant. Yet when combined with humility, and when remaining calm, exercising nerve can make for a very effective, if not tough, negotiation stance. Without nerve you are more likely to become a victim of your own discomfort, lose respect, and ultimately concede more readily. With nerve comes the ability to move position when you are ready and only when it is appropriate.

2. SELF-DISCIPLINE
To understand what to do, and to do that which is appropriate
Self-discipline: it's an everyday term, yet in negotiation it requires you to separate your behavior from your feelings and emotions.

It allows you to be what you need to be and what the situation demands of you, rather than behaving in a way that satisfies your own emotions and levels of comfort. Self-discipline does not require you to be a different person, but to fulfil the role requirements at the time to help you perform. For example, remaining indifferent about the potential of a proposal that has been made may be more appropriate than showing any overt enthusiasm or excitement. Having the self-discipline to resist showing emotion helps you remain calm in appearance. This is not to suggest that you should remain indifferent to all proposals made in your negotiations, but to be disciplined enough that you present the signals you want the other party to read.

Patience and the ability to handle frustration are qualities found in effective negotiators. It is highly frustrating trying to get the other party to agree to something they appear reluctant to do. However, this can be achieved by the use of:

- good timing;
- summarizing;
- repackaging the offer;
- remaining at ease with silence; and
- having the self-control to avoid selling your position or talking inappropriately.

Having achieved this within yourself you need to ensure that, where you are negotiating in a team, the remainder of the team are equally well disciplined.

3. TENACITY

The negotiator's equivalent to stamina

The times you hear the words "no, can't, won't" are the occasions where you will have to turn to "how." Rather than simply concede on the issue, you should examine the rejection from different perspectives to find out what other conditions or circumstances you could introduce as part of maintaining control and managing their expectations. For instance, in tennis if your opponent breaks your serve, you don't give up on the set, you work harder in the next game to regain your position.

There will be times when it is appropriate to hold firm and test the other negotiator's resolve. Tenacity is not only about holding firm on your position but also being prepared to be persistent where you deem it appropriate; perhaps even to employ the "broken record" tactic. This is a tactic to employ when you need to repeat your position time after time until it registers.

It is about having the courage of your convictions when faced with challenges from the other party, which are often used tactically to make you question your own judgment.

Tenacity helps negotiators to work on deals rather than being driven to close on them and conclude agreements prematurely. The more time invested in a deal the more likely you are to create or extract value from it. Few people genuinely enjoy negotiating or can see the value in continuing discussions when the deal is seemingly done. Attitudes such as "We have reached agreement so let's agree now while we're ahead" are held by those who miss the point. It is at this time that "How else can we ensure the contract is delivered?" should be asked. With ever more considerations around how the deal can be tuned, the tenacious negotiator will find value or risk reduction that would otherwise go untouched.

Tenacity helps you to resist capitulation: it's the part of you that enables you to hold your position and not be worn down by the other party. It's an attitude that requires stamina, helping you to seek value right up until you finally agree to conclude the deal.

THE POWER AND VALUE OF EXCLUSIVITY

An American hardware furnishing store that has grown dramatically over the past 10 years prides itself as a destination store. Ninety percent of products are either unique or are supplied as exclusive.

The buying team were considering a new range of cutlery called "The Lymington," which was just about to be launched by William Brown, a specialist from Sheffield, England, who had expected to sell 10,000 sets in the first year of production through their core client base in Europe.

(Continued)

(*Continued*)

Three meetings took place between Mark Franklyn (the account manager for William Brown) and the New York-based buying team. During the first meeting Mark was keen to understand the market opportunity in the US and how this might elevate William Brown's reputation. He explained how the Lymington had already been marketed to existing clients who were keen to place orders. The buying team set out a proposal, which included a 12-month exclusive contract for the design and supply subject to 30% discount based on 10,000 sets.

During the second meeting Mark explained that the increased risk of channeling the entire range through one new client was not in his interest – though he stated that he could provide exclusivity for distribution in the US only. By now the buying team wanted the exclusive deal and had already sold the idea back in to the commercial director in New York. William Brown's board were excited about the US opportunity but wanted to minimize discount levels and ensure the committed volumes would be achieved.

In the third meeting Mark outlined a tough position involving no discounts, 50% payment for the full 10,000 units, 7 days payment terms and the balance drawn down within 6 months. His final point was to insist on confirmation before the end of the week, otherwise he was going ahead with his release into the European market. To William Brown this was an opportunity not only to launch in year 2 into the US but to be associated with the retailer, which would raise credibility. He also wanted to use the attraction of exclusivity to minimize risk. The deal was done. The Lymington sold 30,000 units at a price point that was at a 30% premium, which meant the margin opportunity remained viable to the retailer.

4. ASSERTIVENESS

Tell them what you will do, not what you won't do

The best way to determine the future is to create it.

Being in control of the negotiation primarily comes from being proactive, and demonstrating confidence from being prepared and having a well-defined strategy. Then it's about how well you perform.

The Complete Skilled Negotiator comes across as being firm and in control. Not obnoxious or disrespectful but simply able to say what is necessary in a calm, authoritative manner. This is not about being parental or patronizing in your communication style, but simply being confident in your assertions. This can be a fine line to tread. As an assertive negotiator you need to facilitate the development of the agenda and set out your position. You should focus on the deal and remain open about what is, as well as what is not, possible.

It is worth considering that the outcome of any negotiation can only be influenced by the proposals that you make and flexibility you offer. Therefore, ensure that it is you who is making the proposals. As an assertive negotiator, you will not wait for the other party to make their proposals first. Yes, of course listen to what they have to say to understand where flexibility exists, but ensure that it is your proposal that they are responding to. As an assertive negotiator you should also resist the temptation to conform. You should regard yourself as being "in charge" but yet respect the attitudes, feelings, and views of those you are negotiating with. Being assertive helps you gain respect. Being firm is not to be confused with being rude.

5. INSTINCT

Trust it – you will be right more often than not

Experience and "gut feeling," or what some refer to as a "sixth sense," are traits that effective negotiators refer to as instinct. Instinct helps the Complete Skilled Negotiator:

- to hear not just what is being said but the *meaning* behind the words; and
- to gauge honesty, and sense if the deal is too good to be true or if there is more scope to negotiate.

Your ability to read any situation will allow you to judge your response and respond with counter proposals. If it seems too good to be true, it usually is and you should trust your instinct when you are faced with such a situation.

Most people have good instincts, yet under pressure do not always listen to them. They choose instead to accept the case placed before them and conform rather than challenge. As an effective negotiator you should have the courage of your convictions, challenge anything that does not "feel" right, and always demand clarity before being prepared to progress.

Trust your instinct, otherwise too narrow a view on the bottom line could ultimately provide you with a suboptimized agreement. Price can be incredibly seductive, and those who shut out other considerations, even when the opportunity feels too good to be true, fall foul of listening to and acting on their instinct. The very need to feel as though you got a great deal can be enough to distract you from the logic you might otherwise exercise and has lead to some negotiators agreeing to disastrous deals. Great deals are only so if they are honored and delivered against. Instinctively, you know if you are offered a cheap Rolex watch in a bar by a stranger that the item is unlikely to be from a reputable source. However, how sure would you be if they were in an office dressed in a suit offering a timeshare apartment in Panama? Still suspicious? OK, how about the real-estate agent from a reputable agency who tells you he can sell your house in under a week if you sign with him today?

Instinct usually comes from both experience *and* knowledge, as well as your subconscious observations. The instant evaluation and judgment most people make when they first meet someone else are based on subtle assessments of nonverbal communication and language. The Complete Skilled Negotiator has the ability to make these assessments more consciously as they deliberately analyze the behaviors of the other party.

6. CAUTION

If it seems too good to be true, it probably is

The "action" or interaction, once a negotiation has begun, comes in the form of proposals and counter proposals as the deal starts to take shape.

Picture the high levels of mental energy and the work rate taking place *inside* the heads of two teams of negotiators around the table. Both parties seeking to create or distribute value in the knowledge that if they are too hasty they may miss an implication and, by being seduced on price, they could be entering into an agreement that could carry more risk in the long term. It is during these critical exchanges when reality checks should take place. This is when patience is needed and time should be taken to calculate what has changed.

IF IT SEEMS TOO GOOD TO BE TRUE ... IT USUALLY IS

With the likes of Serena Williams, Beyoncé, and Michelle Obama amongst hundreds of keen celebrities, the nail bar industry has boomed, becoming a $10bn-per-year industry. California alone employs 100,000 nail technicians. Back in 2007 Philip Montone, a Paris-based entrepreneur, hastily set up five bars across the affluent suburbs of Neuilly-sur-Seine. With his experience in the beauty salon industry he was well versed in how middle-class Parisians liked to pamper themselves. Working with a team of nail bar specialists he set about investing. Within a long list of equipment needed were the ultraviolet light units used for curing acrylic. By his calculations, he needed to purchase 20 of these. Following some research he had three suppliers visit his office. All claimed that there was a shortage of supply and there was a 3-month waiting list, such was the surge in growth in the industry.

That evening Philip received a cold call from a supplier direct from Hong Kong. The supplier offered to supply units within 10 days and at the specification Philip was asking for. He negotiated on and secured guaranteed delivery and a 20% discount on the prices before placing the order for $4000. The units arrived 4 days before opening day.

(Continued)

(Continued)

They were everything he had been offered except for one oversight. They were wired for Taiwan at 110 volts and, although they could work with transformers, they would not meet French health and safety regulations.

Philip attracted a great price and delivery, but in his haste, and because of a single oversight, he ended up writing off the total cost. Today you can buy these units on Amazon for as little as $20 a time.

7. CURIOSITY

Asking why because you want and need to know

Gathering information both prior to and during your negotiation is the ultimate way of creating power. Even if you think you understand your market well or you have dealt with someone for many years it's still possible to assume far too much. Some negotiators get caught up with what they need to achieve and the pressures they face, rather than seeking to understand what the other party needs or how things may have changed for them in recent times. Effective questioning used to seek information and uncover facts, data and circumstances, which may be not be obvious or may even be concealed, *must* be a precursor to making any proposal.

- What are their priorities and why?
- What are their time pressures and why?
- What are their options and why?
- How might any of these be changed?

Understanding the situation does not just come from questioning. Researching the other party, talking to others and obtaining credit checks are activities those who want to know and those who are naturally curious will be involved in. It's not an interrogation, but information is power and without insight you will be a weaker negotiator.

8. NUMERICAL REASONING

Know what it's really worth, know what it really costs

Numerical reasoning allows you to consider more easily the "what ifs." Your ability to engineer different trade-off scenarios by performing quick calculations allows you to expose opportunities that might otherwise go unnoticed. This involves linking the value of a risk with the benefit of an opportunity by calculating the incremental upside and then tabling it as a proposal. Although it's a good idea to prepare some proposals ahead of your meeting (following initial discussions), calculating counter proposals and providing alternative solutions during the negotiation with similar or even improved outcomes will come more naturally to those comfortable with numerical reasoning.

Unfortunately, for many, this is not the case. Using simple "ready reckoners" to work out the financial implications of movement is one way of preparing yourself for this. For example, working out the implications of each 1% discount or 1-week extension, or each increase of 500 in unit volume requirements, and having this prepared on a spreadsheet can help you calculate quickly and respond to proposals with a clear understanding of the units and values involved.

Numerical reasoning helps you to calculate options or consequences and prepare and be ready to respond with possible alternatives. It helps discussions and ideas to flow, and also minimizes the number of times the meeting has to adjourn while one party reworks their figures. If you are in doubt, it's highly appropriate to adjourn. If you are ever in doubt about how the value of the deal has or will change as a result of a proposal, you should take whatever time is necessary to understand the implications of entertaining the proposal before moving on.

9. CREATIVITY

Exploring and building on possibilities

Creative solutions not only help resolve deadlock situations but help us to trade off ideas as part of creating more value. By using a creative approach you can link and package variables (volume, timing, specification, etc.) in different ways. Nothing is agreed until everything is agreed, so the creative negotiator is comfortable with degrees of ambiguity as the shape of the deal evolves. It provides you with the chance to introduce options and opportunities rather than trying to work through only those issues in front of you in a disciplined, linear fashion.

Many negotiations involve a broad range of variables and the way these are linked together and are traded against each other provides for the art of creative deal-making. Even when it appears that there are few variables – let's say price, timing, and specification – the creative negotiator will identify other value-adding considerations and turn them into variables ready for negotiation.

If you were buying 50 acres of land from a farmer. The price asked for the land will be important and transparent to both parties. The timing of the availability of the field would allow you to plan out how you intended to make use of the space. Other considerations may include access to the land, fencing, and what the land has been used for in the past. However, the creative negotiator would examine an even broader set of variables as they consider the possible trade offs. What about options in the future on adjoining land, drainage, conditions on how the surrounding land may be used, and contamination? What about letting the land back to the farmer, access for local huntsmen that the farmer is involved with, and so on?

The creative negotiator examines risk, longevity, performance, and the interests of the other party to "fully" scope the parameters of the lifetime of an agreement. The creative negotiator also looks beyond the variables that he or she is measured on as they realize that incremental value may come from elsewhere and often not all components are visible at the outset.

10. HUMILITY

It is people who make agreements and humility that breeds respect
Exercising diplomacy and empathy during negotiations to help manage the appropriate climate sounds like common sense. However, with the tensions that can exist, it's humility that often serves to bring discussions to an adult-to-adult level, cutting through the tactics and gamesmanship in play. Humility removes the need for ego to feature and helps you to

demonstrate your intention of working with the other party, rather than against them, to create a mutually beneficial relationship. Reciprocity ensures that if one party becomes competitive, the other party will mirror this behavior and, as a result, both will find themselves being drawn into positional arguments that become counterproductive. It is your humility that will allow the other party to "win" the argument as they concentrate on the climate and maximizing the total value of the deal from their perspective.

Ultimately, it is not you who is important; it is what is best for the relationship and for the agreement. It's not about competing or about how you feel. Humility requires the removal of personal emotional considerations other than the need to maintain mutual respect with your focus on the agreement. The skills associated with managing climate are well documented under behaviors later in the next chapter. Humility is what sits beneath the behavior. It is a trait that allows you as a negotiator to focus on the quality of the agreement rather than being preoccupied with personalities and personal agendas.

Although it carries risks, having the confidence to admit that you don't know something (where your credibility would not be completely ruined), being open to ideas without appearing influenced, and making the other party feel important are all indicators of humility in play. It's alright not to know all the answers. It is knowing what questions to ask and demonstrating integrity and gravitas that allows those with humility to build the appropriate relationship for the more interdependent deals.

KEY TAKEAWAYS

Some traits will be more reflective of you and your strengths than others. No individual trait will ensure better results, but understanding them and you offers you opportunity to become a truly outstanding negotiator.

- There is going to be some pressure, some tension, maybe even conflict. Control your *nerve*, stick with your plan, never offend, and always remain calm.

- Everything happens for a reason and they will try to influence you and your position. Keep your *self-discipline* and only act as you had planned.
- Some negotiations may wear you down. Your energy levels and *tenacity* will help you to get the best possible deal.
- Take control of your negotiation by exercising your *assertiveness* and self-assurance. Remain firm and yet engaging.
- *Trust your instinct.* If you think it could be too good to be true or if they are not to be trusted, don't continue blindly. Recognize it and act accordingly.
- Before agreeing to any new terms, *exercise caution* by working out the potential consequences or hidden risks.
- Information is power. So, always use your *curiosity* and ask questions throughout your negotiation.
- Make the time to calculate options and alternatives using your *numerical reasoning* before and during the negotiation.
- *Creativity*, building on possibilities, and identifying synergies will help you to problem solve as well as optimize value.
- It is you who will make agreements and your *humility* that will promote the trust needed for your agreements to get across the line.

CHAPTER 5

The Fourteen Behaviors that Make the Difference

"If all you have is a hammer in the toolbox, everything looks like a nail."
Bernard Baruch

The framework for our negotiation standard now starts to unfold. It is time to face yourself and your capability as a negotiator. Your versatility, adaptability, and range of skills will ensure that you can optimize opportunities in all types of negotiations The clock face in Chapter 2 has provided the basis for differentiating the many ways to negotiate. The role of power in Chapter 3 helps us understand how situations and relationships can be manipulated or influenced, meaning that we have to continuously reassess our assumptions. The ten negotiation traits we examined in Chapter 4 provide a framework for self-awareness, enabling us to do that which is appropriate. In this chapter I present the 14 behaviors that enable you to do the appropriate thing at the right time. Together, the traits and behaviors support the competent performance of the Complete Skilled Negotiator.

The fourteen negotiation behaviors capture and describe what it is that you do when negotiating. They make up the varied skills required to perform at different points on the clock face and when employed enable you to be versatile enough to perform in all types of situations. They have been used as a framework for assessing, developing, and supporting negotiations in over 500 corporate businesses around the globe employing the clock face as their "standard" negotiation reference.

1. Think clearly when faced with conflict.
2. Do not allow your sense of fairness to influence behavior.
3. Maintain your self-control, use silence, and manage discomfort.
4. Open extreme yet realistically to shift their expectations.
5. Read their break point.
6. Listen and interpret the meaning behind the words.
7. Plan and prepare using all information available.
8. Question effectively.
9. Always trade concessions effectively and conditionally.
10. Apply analytical skills to manage the value of the deal as the negotiation unfolds.
11. Create and maintain the appropriate climate for trust.
12. Develop and use your agenda to help control the negotiation proceedings.
13. Think creatively to develop proposals which help move the deal forward.
14. Explore options to help gain agreement.

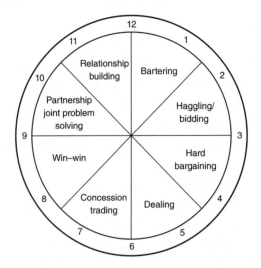

Figure 5.1 The clock face.

The first five behaviors are more commonly, although not exclusively, used on the right-hand side of the clock face (1–6 o'clock negotiations), yet the self-control associated with them can also underpin those behaviors used further around the clock face.

The next three behaviors are based on listening, planning, and questioning, and relate to all positions on the clock face.

The final six behaviors, which build on the former behaviors, help us to perform in more complex agreements where relationship, dependency, and total value are more important.

THE FOURTEEN BEHAVIORS

1. Think clearly when faced with conflict

Everything you do in negotiation requires you to think: if you can't think clearly your performance is going to be compromised. In some ways, it is similar in its definition to the personal trait of nerve (see Chapter 4). The extent of conflict, real or perceived, within a negotiation will vary depending on the strategy being adopted by both parties. The ability to think clearly when faced with conflict is one that will serve any negotiator well at any point on the clock face.

Imagine that you receive a letter outlining a price increase of 5%. It is unexpected and comes with a limp excuse citing market conditions. Your first reaction is disbelief and then anger. You reach for the phone and then place it down as you reflect on your approach. You need to think clearly and consider your approach. You need to control your emotions and commence negotiations in control of yourself, if not yet of the situation. The risk is that your emotional reactions could confuse or cloud your ability to perform in such circumstances which clearly is not in your best interests.

Thinking clearly involves not allowing the other party to make you feel as though it is you who does not understand the market and who needs to move. Never agree to anything unless you understand it. In negotiation, nothing is agreed until everything is agreed, so make sure you have not missed anything before agreeing. It also means standing up to anyone exercising arrogance as they attempt to manipulate your thinking – unless you want them to think they are doing so because it serves your interests.

When there are major consequences at stake, or serious time pressures in play and there is an obligation on you to perform, you will inevitably experience pressure. Depending on how much pressure, your ability to think clearly may be affected. It's your ability to hold your nerve and accommodate pressure that will differentiate your performance, especially in hard bargaining negotiations.

MANAGING CONFLICTING POSITIONS

It was to be the third meeting and negotiations had been progressing well. All but three issues had now been agreed and both teams were starting to anticipate the contract start date which was within a week and was one of the outstanding issues. There was clearly urgency around the work needing to be done. The evening before the meeting, an email arrived with the Marketing Director's "final position" detailing the final three points, with a deadline of 10.30am the following morning.

The third meeting was due to start at 9am that morning. The team from the branding agency arrived and the climate was cool. Rather than respond to the email, they re stated their own position and then explained that they were not empowered to negotiate any further. Once stated, they said nothing. They did not mention or give the email any recognition.

The Marketing Director said: "You know we can't afford your fees as they stand." The branding agency manager held his hand out and offered a final 2.5% discount. He had been asked for 10%. The room was quiet and remained so for 2 minutes. It felt like 20. Both nerve and silence remained as the Marketing Director had to make his mind up. Was he going to conclude or walk? The deal was done. Rather than capitulate or deadlock, the agency manager had thought through the situation and decided to provide just enough movement to demonstrate that he wanted the business. By managing the conflicting positions and tension in the room the branding agency were able to agree the deal.

In practice
- Gather your thoughts and remove any emotion from your thinking; if you do not do this you will lose composure and will more likely underperform.
- Demand clarity as a condition of continuing.
- Remain focused on your purpose at all times.
- Control the negotiation by restating your position and letting them do the talking.
- If you are not sure about the deal or what it adds up to, then take time out. You can always return once you have taken time to consider your options.

2. Do not allow your sense of fairness to influence behavior

Fairness has no place in negotiation as it cannot be measured objectively. What's fair to you may not seem fair to the other party so it cannot be relied on as a basis for seeking agreement.

However, the perception of fairness is important where you need balanced cooperation with the other party and where you need to work with them on an ongoing basis. But "fair" is a subjective word and a relative term. You offer one person a price of $40 and they think that's a fair price. You offer another person a price of $40 and they think it's unfair. The first has been used to paying $45 elsewhere and thinks they have a good deal and the price is fair. The second has never purchased before but is expecting a price of $35, so is not happy.

Similarly, fairness is not the answer to conflict. Opting to split differences straight down the middle, for example, is not negotiating: it is compromising. The need to exhibit fairness often leads inexperienced negotiators to accept the 50:50 offer. This is because it feels "fair," when they should make further counter proposals to provide less costly solutions. So rather than grabbing the deal with the final 50:50 split, for example, why not offer a further conditional proposal that costs you less than 50% of the difference?

The more you try to be fair, the more your "generosity" will be taken advantage of. Most people will not live by the same value set as you. They may simply be more callous or irrational about how they go about trading. One thing is for sure: they are out to maximize profit and, if you make it easy for them, it will be to the detriment of your interests.

Perversely, people who do operate in a fair way during negotiations can in fact be perceived as unfair. For example, in a hard bargaining situation at 4 o'clock someone may decide not to ask for more than they expect in the first instance to avoid offending the other party. Their sense of fairness results in them feeling uncomfortable with the prospect of rejection, which would be likely in the event of them opening with a very high or low offer. The other party, however, expecting to negotiate, will want them to move from their opening position in order to gain some satisfaction. The first party is left with two options: either to give away value that they cannot afford to (because they have already opened on their break point); or to say "no" and not move. This in itself could lead to a perception of stubbornness, unfairness and, potentially, deadlock.

Firm is not rude, tough is not nasty. Liked is not respected. When hard bargaining, nice people don't get good deals.

In practice
- Aim to look for the optimum solution rather than simply a fair one.
- Remember that the easy, fair route to splitting the difference is rarely the optimum way to the best deal for all concerned.
- If the other party offers to split down the middle, it usually means that they would probably accept less.
- If you concede they will want more – all trade-offs should be conditional.

3. Maintain your self-control, use silence, and manage discomfort

This competitive behavior might be regarded as unacceptable in many relationships, but when you are trying to move the other person's position, self-control and silence are the most powerful of behaviors to conduct.

During a hard bargaining negotiation at 4 o'clock, for example, there is inevitably a conflict in positions: Tension and sometimes even emotion can run high. For most, it's uncomfortable but for the trained negotiator it is part of the territory. The stronger your self-control, the more power you will attract attract as the conversation unfolds.

Negotiation has less to do with talking and more to do with listening. You should let the other party:

- sell their position;
- explain their position;
- promote all the benefits; and
- explain why they need an agreement "today."

Negotiation is silence and to master this is to maintain self-control and manage the resulting discomfort. Information is power and the more they talk the more powerful you will become.

Conversely, if the other person remains silent and you feel obliged to respond, don't. Don't pay the price by instantly conceding as you attempt to remove your discomfort, because if you speak too early, that is what will happen. *If you have nothing to say, say nothing.* They are thinking. Let them think. If you speak to fill the gap, you will probably end up compromising your position by offering further information or even by implying that there is room for movement.

What you think is important and need to say will usually work against you. A local café always offered a window display full of delicious cakes sold by the slice. People rarely walked passed without admiring the range of cakes presented in the window. Trade was always good due to the reputation of the cakes. The cakes were sourced from a local cake maker who supplied 15 large cakes each day. The margin was very healthy for the café. The price they paid for each cake averaged £20. The supply agreement was informal, with orders placed each week and daily deliveries arriving by 8.30am.

The cake maker asked for a meeting with Mark, the café manager who was authorized to purchase all stock requirements. The relationship was a strong and a familiar one, which was by now in its third year. The cake maker demanded a 15% price increase with immediate effect and handed over the new price list to the manager. Mark examined the note and said nothing. She then started to explain why, citing ingredient cost increases. Mark continued to say nothing. The cake maker then said that there had not been a price increase for over a year. He agreed with her. It was a fact. "I provide you with highest quality cakes, which keeps your café busy all year round," she said. Mark agreed. He finally turned to the cake maker and said, "If you maintain your current terms and service level we will renew our agreement with you for a further year. Please let me know what you want to do by tomorrow morning."

He did not argue with her case or seek to negotiate over the 15%. He listened, remained calm, and restated his position. With no justification and without being rude. He remained "in charge." And she ultimately accepted the deal.

In practice
- Let the other party do the talking and focus your attention first on what they are saying, rather than thinking too much about how to respond.
- Listen to what the other party is saying in order to establish how far they will move from their current position.
- If you are not ready to make your proposal, either ask a question or say nothing.

4. Open extreme yet realistically to shift their expectations

To open extreme is simple enough, as you just state your proposal. The fear of the predictable rejection, however, results in many feeling uncomfortable with stating it in the first place. Because of the fear of the reaction we are expecting, we risk losing our composure. Rather than saying "my price is $50," some will say something like, "I'm looking for around $50," which instantly suggests it's negotiable. If it's worth $100 to you, offer

$50. We know they are going to reject the offer but that's part of the process.

You can't change or remove this feeling of being uncomfortable so you need to get used to it or find ways to accommodate it. To do this, think about it as a process that you are involved in. The process will do three things for you.

1.   First, it will help you to position your offer appropriately.
2.   Second, it will help you to counter the position of the other party.
3.   Third, it will ensure that you provide the other party with the satisfaction of having got a better deal than they believed was originally available.

Your opening position or proposal should be extreme enough for them not to accept it, but not so extreme that they choose to walk away, concluding the conversation there and then. If your opening position is too extreme, the other party may conclude that you are wasting their time, are not serious or credible and move on. Your offer also has to be realistic if they are to stay engaged.

For example, if you wanted to buy something for $200 and they are asking $300, you might negotiate them down, depending on the circumstances. But if you were attempting to finish at $200 by opening at $25, then they would probably walk away.

The purpose of opening extreme is to create an anchor from which to move. If you have control over your own sense of fairness and can manage your discomfort, then you will be able to do this. Assuming the other party is still talking to you, you are now in a proactive position that allows movement on your part, given that you will have taken up an opening position outside of their break point.

You can wipe their extreme openers off the table by attaching equally ludicrous conditions to their price. Imagine a seller said to you "the price is $150." You respond with: "I can agree, subject to payment installments over 3 years and that the item is guaranteed for the duration of the payment plan." In negotiation you never need to say no. You can always re-engineer the variables in such a way that you can say yes and yet with your terms which off set or counter the offer being made. Simply attach conditions that offset the implications of saying yes. Also, you never have to, nor should you, lie in negotiations. There is no need to if you understand the process you are involved in. The process of opening extreme is simply that – a process – and is usually employed in the hard bargaining context. By offering $50 you are not lying, you are simply making an offer by telling them what you will agree to.

During tough one-dimensional negotiations, it is important to recognize that you can get a great price and yet a lousy deal. Never get so into attacking their position. It will usually result in you losing sight of your own position. An antique clock collector negotiated an amazingly low price on a clock at an antiques fair. The seller said that it needed "some attention" as it was not working. However, he was seduced by the price he had been able to agree and bought it. That was 5 years ago. The clock has now been through three different repairs, costing the collector the asking price over again. After each repair the clock worked for less than a week. It now sits at the back of his workshop.

If it appears too good to be true, it usually is.

In practice
- Ensure your opening position is extreme enough for them not to accept it – but not so extreme that they will immediately walk away.
- Make your position credible by cutting out any soft exposing statements: avoid the use of words like "around," "in the region of," "I was hoping for …," "we were expecting …"
- Use a non-verbal reaction to their opening position – tactically known as the professional flinch, this is designed to clearly demonstrate to the other party your surprise at their position.
- Apply self-control when making your offer, state your figure – then shut up.
- Learn to be at ease with silence.

5. Read their break point

In any hard bargaining negotiation, you should define your break point first. That is:

- The point at which you have other options that you could take.
- The point at which the deal is not viable.
- The point at which you will walk, rather than do business.

This is not your objective or a measure, just a fail-safe position. Its only purpose is to prevent you from agreeing to a deal that, in the cold light of day, is just not viable. Your job when hard bargaining is to finish the deal as close to their break point as possible. Therefore, your first task is to work out where you think this is, and then open extreme and yet realistic on the other side of it assuming of course you are hard bargaining.

You can read the other party's limits through:

- the types of proposals they make;
- the language they use to justify their movements;
- the timescales they are working to; and
- the size and frequency of their concessions or counter proposals.

This can help you to identify their break point. Their opening position and response to yours will help you plot where you think they may settle. Under pressure people often say (without realizing) the exact opposite of what they actually mean to say. For example, if they say "we once paid $60 an hour for this and would not do it again," they are saying this not to you but to themselves. Even *they* do not believe it. It's their denial that drives this behavior so listen to what they are saying. If they were not prepared to go to $60 an hour they would not feel the need to state it.

Reading their break point is about reading the situation based on a combination of information, questioning, and reading of their actions. All should help you to establish how much they need the deal and how far they will go. Time can play a role here. Where negotiations go on for weeks and months, many will agree to offers that would have been totally unacceptable during the earlier stages of the negotiation. Sometimes the negotiation process serves to wear them down; it could be that other options they thought they had have dissolved or that the time and energy spent negotiating would be better spent elsewhere, so they conclude the deal. Sometimes circumstances change over the duration of the negotiation, throwing up more options or alternatives and therefore influencing the flow of events.

Under great pressure some have even been known to capitulate and forget their break point altogether. How many times have you heard of people who have come out of an auction having paid far more than the limit they had set themselves because they got caught up in the heat of the moment?

In practice
- Remember you are negotiating with a person, not a company, and each will carry a set of circumstances that will be unique to them.
- Assess where their break point is by examining previous agreements (if you have dealt with them before), researching the market, and speaking to competitors.
- Identify the issues of high value to them and try to establish the issues in which they are prepared to be more flexible.
- One way of working out your own break point is to define your Best Alternative to a Negotiated Agreement (BATNA).
- Test your own assumptions by stating them as facts and waiting for their response.

6. Listen and interpret the meaning behind the words
There is so much to be learned through what we see and hear. The phrase "getting into their head" has as much to do with getting *out* of our own head. Rather than concentrating on our own thoughts and feelings, we need to consciously turn our attentions to theirs.

Watch them, watch for the signals. This can include phrases such as, "well that wasn't as much as we were hoping for," "I can't go that far," or "I was looking for a higher figure," all of which suggest they are in the process of revising their expectations.

There is so much to be learned through what we see and hear. "Getting into their head" has as much to do with getting *out* of our own head. Rather than concentrating on our own thoughts and feelings, we need to consciously turn our attentions to theirs.

Listening to what the other party says is only part of the skill involved in reading and understanding them. Look for inconsistencies in the way they attempt to justify their position. The more they talk, the weaker they are feeling. If they start to sell the benefits of their offer during the negotiation, they are feeling weak. Remember that the same will apply in the way they read your behavior.

- **Establish how firm their offer or proposal is.** Try to observe the "soft exposing giveaways:" "I was looking for around $500, if that sounds OK?" This is not a firm offer; it's a very obvious example of someone feeling uncomfortable tabling their opening offer. Often we are given less obvious hints, yet there can still be clues within how their proposal is stated. Try to listen for what is said and how it is said.
- **Focus on listening to the questions asked.** For example, if they ask you if it is available today, or if you can pay cash, rather than simply answering those questions, you should think about *why* they are asking such a question, and perhaps ask in return why this is important to them. If you are wrapped up in your own head, then you will miss the opportunity to qualify the things that are important to them.
- **Once you have listened, stop and interpret what the information offers.** This should be before you feel obliged to respond. For many, the time taken feels uncomfortable, but the new information needs time to be considered. If they are selling and are opening with $500, where might their break point be? Think about this before you respond. The ability to actively listen for information that may help progress the negotiation, rather than using the time available to think about what you want to say next, leans heavily on the negotiator's trait of curiosity (trait 7, Chapter 4).

In practice
- As a Complete Skilled Negotiator, understanding their position, priorities, interests, pressures, and needs is a critical part of your job.
- The value of listening is far greater than that which can be achieved by what you have to say.
- Listen and interpret their true position. How much do they need this deal? How many options do they really have? How dependent are they on an early decision?
- Think about *why* they are asking a particular question, and ask in return why this is important to them.
- Actively listen for information that will help you to progress the negotiation, rather than thinking about what you want to say next.

7. Plan and prepare using all information available

There is a direct correlation between successful negotiations, however measured, and the time invested in preparation. Planning can be as simple as building an agenda, or as complex as managing many stakeholders involved in multiple negotiations around the world requiring a detailed strategy and tactical analysis for all concerned. It is important to emphasize just how critical planning is as a discipline and as a behavior, as so few managers I have met take the time to plan properly, taking the attitude that they can still perform without it. (This is explored in greater depth in the final chapter of this book.)

Insight, options, confidence, direction, knowledge, and control can all be gained from preparation using all information available. An attitude of familiarity with the situation or relationship can result in no or poor preparation. You should never "wing it." We all work under pressure and the task of planning can often be minimized or even forgotten in favor of "more urgent" tasks. You need to take the time to plan. It has been proven time after time that effective negotiators plan in advance.

You should plan:

- what questions to ask;
- what position or statement to open with;
- what type of agenda to use;

- how to present your opening position;
- how to respond;
- what information they will need;
- when and where the meeting will be held;
- who needs to be involved; and
- when discussions will commence, and much more.

Some negotiations can take weeks or even months to prepare for. When the stakes are high, each and every possibility should be considered. Even routine negotiations should be given as long as necessary to work through the issues, values, and possibilities. Your planning should help you develop insight, confidence, and structure. All of this will help you take more control of your negotiation.

THE POSITIVE EFFECT OF METICULOUS PLANNING

An ice cream franchisee, Mario, had held a contract to supply hotels and restaurants in the Milan area on behalf of a major, high-quality, branded ice cream manufacturer. The arrangement had been in place for 15 years and had evolved into "an interpretation" of terms away from the original contract. Even the original contract was "loose" and provided the manufacturer with no real protection.

Mario's operation had gone largely unnoticed by the board of the supplier, a global brand, leaving him free to trade as he felt fit. The time had come to re-negotiate the contract, which presented the global brand with a sensitive situation. They were not at liberty to cancel the contract or change many of the terms without mutual consent. The franchisee had built up such strong relationships that there was a real risk of damage, both in brand reputation and in financial terms.

The senior account team took 3 days to plan a strategy, using numerous insights about Mario's business and importantly the interests of those who ran the business. The changes they needed to make included limiting the types of establishments that their branded ice

(Continued)

(Continued)

cream could be sold into. Mario's operation was currently supplying retail and leisure parks, which were undermining the premium branding of the ice cream. The team analyzed the dependency in the relationship and then mapped out a process. They had been given 3 months by their board to gain agreement.

The first phase involved qualifying a range of interests and assumptions before structuring an agenda for future negotiations. The planning was meticulous, phased, and patient. They sought to understand the true sensitivities and how these might be addressed. They sought to understand the Mario family and other stakeholders in the business and where their interests lay. Following the 3 days of preparation they held an "exploration" meeting with Mario and his team. This was a continuum of their own planning process. Having advised through this negotiation, I observed the hundreds of hours of time and effort that went into the preparation, which ultimately resulted in a re-drawing of the contract that traded off improved terms for Mario in return for a narrowed definition of territory. In turn this enabled the global brand to initiate a nationwide branding campaign re-launching their premium brand.

In practice

- The time to start getting into their head is during your preparation.
- Focus your attention on each variable you are likely to discuss and be precise about the information you need or questions you plan to ask.
- Keep a record to simplify future planning.
- Involve others in your preparation – it will strengthen your discipline to plan in the first place, as well as keeping you grounded and objective in your assessments.
- Plan the agenda and map out the variables you can employ.
- Ensure you understand the values of the trade-offs involved against each of the variables from inside their head.

8. Question effectively

In March 2007, a senior government official in the UK confessed that his biggest regret was not challenging the assumptions being made about the existence of weapons of mass destruction prior to the invasion of Iraq. He admitted that more questions could have prompted more answers, which may have altered the course of history.

The following approach, STROB, enables you to plan out how you can extract more information than might otherwise be forthcoming. It helps you to create five open-ended questions which enable you to open up or expand your knowledge and understanding.

1. Examine broadening the **SCOPE** of the agreement as part of broadening or narrowing your relationship. This could include considering the longevity of the relationship, dependency, risk, or other factors, which create greater scope for maximizing value.
2. List the **TERMS** you think will feature and their relative value to them. This could include their basic requirements, issues, or could be related to how the individual negotiator will be measured.
3. List any issues they or you may regard as **RISK** related. This could include time scales, third-party relationships, market assumptions, etc.
4. List any/all of the **OPTIONS** you believe they may have if your negotiations run into difficulties. In the event of deadlock what would they do?
5. List the potential **BARRIERS**, issues, or objections that are likely to be presented.

The STROB technique is used by converting your questions into order of importance, listing your top ten, and using these during the exploratory phase of your discussions.

For example, making use of "what if" questions to establish how the other party might respond to different scenarios and their attitude to risk can help during your exploratory meetings. They can also be used to help identify priorities and the value the other party places on certain issues. "What if we order 50,000?", "What if we order 100,000?", "So what if we order 600,000 then?" – these are questions that will help you to understand the economies of volume. Taken a step further, you can start to question timings, payment terms, and all other variables with "what ifs" to help establish how their cost base is made up, what is easier for them to agree on, and where flexibility lies within their list of interests.

As the Complete Skilled Negotiator, you will have the confidence to be flexible and to use a combination of questioning styles in order to extract the most useful information (see the following box).

QUESTION TYPES

- **Contact questions** help you to establish rapport: "How have you been since we last met? Did you have a good holiday? How is business?"
- **Probing questions** help you to seek further information: "What do you think about your competitor's latest activities?"
- **Interrogative questions** help you to encourage them to think about solutions for themselves: "Why is that important to you?"
- **Comparative questions** help you to explore in detail: "What has business been like since the introduction of product A? How have things changed since your new promotion began?"
- **Extension questions** challenge: "How do you mean? How else could we do that? What are you thinking of specifically? What do you mean when you say …? How can you be sure of that?"
- **Opinion seeking questions** test their knowledge and thinking: "How do you feel about …? What do you think about …? What are your views on …?"
- **Hypothetical questions** help you to test their knowledge and thinking: "What if we were to order 500 units? What if we included all the costs? What if I paid you in advance?"
- **Reflective/summary questions** draw ideas together and test their understanding, and summarize what has been said: "So, you think that we need to introduce this new range? You think that the product will achieve X? As I understand it, you reckon that you can deliver it?"

- **Closing questions** help you to secure agreement: "When should we start – during May or at the beginning of June? I can deliver on the first or second week of that month; which would suit you best? How much?"
- **Mirror questions** serve to reverse the question and confirm the point: "We think we can deliver this for you." "You think you can deliver this?"
- **Leading questions** help you to secure a desired answer. "You can't deny that …? Isn't it a fact that …? You wouldn't say that …? It's a great offer, isn't it?"
- **Rhetorical questions** help you to prevent them from saying anything as they do not require an answer: "Do we really want to do that? And how did that happen?" *Implying that you already know.*
- **Multiple questions** help you to gain agreement to a package: "You did say that you could meet the deadline? Oh, and you will meet our specification and, ah, by the way, you can do this for us can't you?"
- **Closed questions** help you to establish specific facts/information: "Will you do this? Have you the ability to deliver? Can you meet our requirements? Do you need help with this offer?"

In practice

- Use the STROB technique to put your questions into order of importance.
- Make a conscious effort to work on the different questioning types in order to maintain control.
- If they are reluctant to answer, try asking your question in a different way.
- Be careful to avoid being seen as interrogating – you're likely to attract suspicion and resistance.
- Also be wary that you can sometimes give away your own interests unintentionally by the way you ask questions.

9. Always trade concessions effectively and conditionally

Every trade you make should be considered and conditional.

The aim of trading is to build more value for your business as a result of each trade. As there are no rules in negotiation, you can, in theory, offer anything that has a value to them, providing it is a reciprocated move. Whatever they want, they can have, in return for something you want. Each trade then should be designed to provide you with a net gain. In practice you will of course want to weigh up any variable traded as the implications of trading it may be broader than simply its financial value.

Imagine an international footballer in the transfer market about to move club. The negotiation involves the player's agent and the chairman of the football club. The agenda is made up of a transfer fee, a signing on fee, length of contract, salary and bonuses, and a range of performance-related incentives and obligations the player has to meet. Variables could also include the phasing of payments in relation to appearances, number of goals scored, or whether they appear for their country. Each variable will feature as part of a set of conditional trade-offs. The club, having chosen their man, want to ensure that they get maximum value from his services. Meanwhile the player may be looking for maximum income or flexibility within the contract, known as "personal terms." Each of the variables can be adjusted as part of the negotiation that follows and the process involved is that of trading concessions.

When trading concessions you therefore need to identify through your planning and questioning what is important to them. This will help you to build proposals involving concessions that are the least cost to you, but represent a greater value to them. In return, your condition is that they provide movement that improves the value of the deal for you. This sounds rational, fair, and transparent but usually it's not. What they offer will be no more than they absolutely have to and usually this is something of a minimum cost to them.

Understanding the implications of their offer is critical if you are to assess what you want in return. Your creativity can work wonders when you move away from price only, and focus on total cost or total value.

You can only trade effectively when you understand or gauge the value of an issue in their terms. Part of this you may know from understanding your market, and part may be from any history you may have with the other party. Remember, low-cost and high-value trade-offs should be worked through as part of your preparations before negotiating begins. Work out the trade-offs. Work out your potential moves. Remember, generosity engenders greed. Nothing is free in this world and if you start providing unconditional concessions, the other party will either get suspicious or just plain greedy.

In practice
- Identify what is important to the other party through your planning and questioning.
- Build proposals that involve concessions of least cost to you, but greater value to them.
- Use "What if …?" questions to explore the value and measure reactions to particular suggestions.
- Always place your condition first, rather than the concession (i.e. "If you … then we …") as they will be less likely to interrupt you in order to hear what's in it for them.
- Be creative when identifying options for trading – change the shape of the deal rather than focusing on what can't be done.

10. Apply analytical skills to manage the value of the deal as the negotiation unfolds

As a negotiation unfolds, the total value or cost of a deal often becomes more complex as the number of issues increases. This especially includes negotiations that involve a number of variables; each of which need to be agreed and many of which will be interrelated. Let's say you are agreeing a contract that involves office furniture. There are a range of issues to be agreed. You make a proposal that consists of the shortening of payment terms in return for a lower up-front payment or deposit. In being able to track the progress of your negotiation you need to understand the cost or value of each variable to both you and the other party.

You need to calculate the saving for them if payment is settled over a shorter period of time and how they will value a lower deposit, sometimes literally as the negotiation is unfolding. Of course, this goes hand in hand with understanding these values or costs from your own perspective. Using your analytical skills enables you to understand the implications of their response and work out what your next proposal might be:

"We will accept the lower deposit subject to you reducing your payment schedule from your proposed 12 months to 9 months."

How would this affect the total value of the agreement? Should you now park this issue and examine how other terms can be introduced as part of the conversation?

Understanding the implications of trades is critical to working through possibilities and opportunities as we effectively "engineer the deal." That is not to say that you have to be lightning quick with figures or that you have to be highly analytical to work through more complex agreements. You simply have to ensure that, through the time you take or the way you delegate or automate (sometimes using spreadsheets) such activities, you are clear about the decisions you are taking.

The less tangible an issue is, the more difficult it can be to value the trade. Some examples might be:

- the changing of opt-out clauses;
- agreement to a testimonial recommendation;
- flexibility in completion dates; and
- the offer of exclusivity.

Understanding how to value these types of implications within an agreement is important if you are to trade them effectively. The cost may be little to you and yet hold a significant value to the other party.

During your negotiations, track your and their proposals by documenting them, so you can monitor each issue's progress and movement. Track what their last proposal was and what the value of the deal equates to for you. Make use of spreadsheets to analyze "what if" scenarios and for tracking proposals, especially when it's an existing contract being renegotiated and the issues under review are consistent.

If, despite this, you struggle with the figures, take your time. Take time out or take someone with you to the negotiation as your "figures person." If you become wrapped up in figures, you will not be in control of the negotiation. If you don't understand the figures, you are in danger of agreeing to something that may prove regrettable.

In the commercial arena, you are negotiating over resources, interests, priorities, preferences, even prejudices. There is a broad range of both tangible and intangible issues, all of which carry a perception of value. Then of course there is money. If you are not aware of the consequences of your proposals, then you are not in control. Make it your business to qualify the worth of all the issues under discussion that you are responsible for negotiating.

In practice
- Ensure that you understand the implications of the other party's response in order to work out what your next proposal might be.
- Track your and the other party's proposals so that you can monitor each issue's progress and movement.
- If you struggle with figures, take your time, or ensure you take someone as your "figures person".
- Make it your business to qualify the worth of all the issues under discussion.

11. Create and maintain the appropriate climate for trust
This is critical if the other party is to accept your ideas as being genuinely helpful and to consider the options you bring to the table. Remember, you are responsible for their feelings and the atmosphere during the negotiation. If they do not feel the ideas being tabled are in the interest of mutual progress, they simply will not entertain them.

Where real or perceived conflict of interests exists, trust can be difficult to come by as each party gravitates towards protecting its own interests. The other party may not be as open-minded as you or the balance of power (being in their favor) may mean that they do not need to be so. It takes two to tango. If they choose to hard bargain, you must be prepared to backtrack and adjust your strategy. Drive at a broader agenda with the aim of building a sustainable agreement rather than engaging in a bruising battle over price.

In a sustainable relationship (9–12 o'clock on the clock face) it is critical to maintain a basis where constructive dialogue can take place without suspicion or the need to compete. Remain cooperative, present creative proposals, and use statements that help promote progress. Adopt a broader perspective and an acceptance of the longer-term benefits that a relationship based on trust and respect will bring.

At 4 o'clock on the clock face you are hard bargaining and are without relationship constraints – you can be tough. However, when there is a high level of dependency between you, you not only need to be cooperative but should recognize what cooperation provides you with: a basis for creating more value. Your plan to maximize profits remains the same. The way you achieve this is by working with the other party, and changes as you move around to beyond 6 o'clock.

To gain trust, you have to earn it and this takes time and patience. One way to help achieve this during meetings is by offering information in a controlled and considered manner. The act of sharing information is important to both parties, as it demonstrates that you are prepared to be open and hence, by implication, to be trusted. Therefore, you need to organize and manage what information you are prepared to offer. This is an important part of any negotiator's preparation.

Creating the appropriate climate for trust may require you to do something or be someone you are not. This is where the "conscious negotiator" comes into his or her own. They recognize the egos involved, recognize how the other party wants to be treated, and present a cooperative front. They attack the problems and not the people by ensuring the climate in the room remains conducive to building the agreements.

In practice

- Trust takes time to build so patience is needed; yet it can be destroyed in a moment if you cross the other party.
- Offer information in a controlled and considered manner to demonstrate that you are prepared to be open and can be trusted.
- Drive at a broader agenda with the aim of building a sustainable agreement rather than engaging in a bruising battle over price.

12. Develop and use your agenda to help control the negotiation proceedings

The agenda is effectively a working document for all parties involved, which helps to shape and control negotiation proceedings. It is there to provide transparency around those negotiable variables that will contribute towards the total value of the agreement.

Further, agreeing on an agenda before the meeting helps ensure that it is "owned" by all involved. Agreeing on the agenda alone can sometimes require a negotiation in itself. If you impose an agenda on the other party, they are more likely to be dismissive and challenging of the issues. Ultimately, both parties agree that all items in need of consideration are listed, and agree that all parties will work from it.

Imagine contracting with a PR firm. Having narrowed down the options to the final two firms, you decide to enter into negotiations to find out where you are most likely to attract the greatest value from. Now, PR at the best of times is a challenging service to measure. However, the basic terms of any agreement will need to feature as part of your agenda. This could include:

- a retainer fee;
- notice period;
- length of contract;
- range of services;
- PR training provided;
- contact requirements; and
- payment terms.

Already we have seven issues to be discussed on the agenda and from these there will be further issues relating to performance, compliance, and risks linked to each of these seven. The broader the agenda, the more comprehensive your considerations, and the greater the scope for shaping the deal and ultimately building a higher-value agreement.

Some parties choose to outline their entire offer from the outset. Some tendering processes demand your opening position across all variables. Even though you may be in possession of this information you need not be drawn into responding to them all at once. Try to trade off no more than three issues at a time. Any more makes it difficult for them to calculate and, worse still, confusing to understand.

Watch out for hidden agenda points or "red herrings" introduced by the other party with the aim of trading off against them. In doing so, they expect to gain some leverage on issues that are important to them. Where new issues appear on the agenda, set out to qualify their legitimacy. Conversely you may choose to let the other party win some of the lower-cost issues and gain the leverage you need to secure those issues that are both important and of high value to you.

Even if you list a draft agenda on a flip chart in the room minutes before your meeting, you have created the illusion that you are prepared. This provides a basis to explore the variables that will need agreeing with the other party in a more collaborative manner.

In practice
- The broader the agenda, the greater scope there is for shaping the deal.
- Aim to trade off no more than three issues at a time.
- Watch out for hidden agenda points or "red herrings" introduced by the other party with the aim of trading off against them.
- Position price, fee, or cost about halfway down your agenda – too early and it can promote unnecessary friction; too late and it could limit room for maneuver.
- If you are going to "lose" or concede on an issue, then trade it conditionally and reluctantly – if it is truly important to the other party, they may give ground to secure it.

13. Think creatively to develop proposals that help move the deal forward
Thinking creatively– that is to say thinking around the issues and possibilities that might not have been considered or traded before – can move the negotiation forwards. Picture yourself as a sculptor: designing, forming, shaping in an artistic manner. Stand back and examine your progress from different angles and perspectives. You are involved in carving out something of much greater value than the sum total of the materials involved. The creative negotiator interprets the possibilities before them and regards the challenge in hand as one of creating value.

In an online consumer situation, for example, you are usually presented with pages of terms and conditions that consumers are unlikely to ever read. They are presented as a "take it or leave it" contract offering most little real choice. However, in business, the same tactics are employed by procurement teams who often miss the opportunity to negotiate around terms more creatively in order to optimize value.

An English sparkling wine company were raising funds through a crowd funding scheme, offering a return on investment through a 5-year bond, with "fixed terms and conditions" attached.

As expected, I received the standard terms and conditions. It was made up of four pages of text in font size 6. The assumption was that I would not read it and that the terms were a given. It covered everything from liabilities, confidentiality, payment terms, contract amendments, copyright protection, and so on. From this, I identified 23 variables (apart from price) that I decided to discuss – some offering the potential for more flexibility and some for opportunity (e.g. increased investment stake at a later stage).

The company owner agreed to a meeting. At first the owner was hesitant to engage. I am sure he had had easier conversations with other investors. However, after agreeing on the first two conditional trades, the conversation continued. The agreement we struck through some creative trade-offs offered me a deal that I was truly married to by the time I had finished and an opportunity for the sparkling wine company to sell their wines through another business I am involved in.

Sometimes you just have to tell the other party what is important; otherwise you are not providing them with the opportunity to make things possible. Detailed exploratory discussions can offer tremendous opportunities to build agendas, which reflect every part of the deal including the risks, performance, compliance, quality, opportunity, communication, and many other important components of the relationship.

The ability to remain open-minded and use creative or lateral thinking during negotiation is difficult for many people. It is competitiveness, pride, a need to maintain face, and even ego that prevents many from being open. This result can be a dogmatic approach aimed at minimizing risk and sometimes "winning."

In negotiation the lateral thinking patterns associated with creativity are at direct odds with those emotions experienced during moments of perceived conflict. Where conflict exists, we are more inclined to batten down the hatches and are more likely to focus on protecting our position. By adopting a mindset driven by "under what circumstances" we become much more able to explore and be creative rather than being bound by insecurity.

In practice
- Understand what is really important to them and why.
- Differentiate the people from the issues.
- Extend your mutual agenda to create more possible variables.
- Consider any risks involved and trade these off where possible.
- Identify low-cost, high-value trade-off opportunities.

14. Explore options to help gain agreement

Try to resist the temptation to say no. The challenges and frustrations presented in negotiations are there to test us. Deadlock is an option but only after every possible option has been exhausted. Where peace talks can take years, merger and acquisition negotiations months, the work involved in searching for common areas where agreement can be struck comes from the persistence of those involved. There has to be a belief that there is a solution to be found. The trait of tenacity (Chapter 4) helps the

Complete Skilled Negotiator to explore options continuously, keep the agreement and relationships on track, and deliver the possible deal from what once seemed, at best, unlikely.

Although it's appropriate to remain on your guard, if you are able to park your suspicion and search for alternatives and other conditional options, you will surprise yourself just how many times a last-minute solution can be found. By seeing the whole picture and the possible links that can be made, you will be able to bring in possibilities exploring options that may not have been considered before.

A merger of two software companies is under way and it's a week before the final deal. Documents are due to be signed, yet conversations are continuing over the management structure of the new enlarged business. Both CEOs believe they have the credentials to lead and could best serve the new larger group.

This leads to a deadlock situation, placing the merger at risk. Identifying with this situation, the finance broker introduces a facilitator to "help identify a solution," who starts by saying "I respect what you both feel may be at stake here and the extent to which your respective companies will be looking for reassurances. However, if we are not able to resolve this issue, everyone will lose. It is your responsibility to explore options and identify a solution for the greater good. Can we agree on that to start with?"

They did. The situation was complicated. There were careers at stake. A list of interests were drawn up. None were financial. With interests revealed and both parties prepared for the better good to work on their interests rather than against the other, a deal was struck. One took up the role of Chairman and the other CEO.

In practice
- Convert thoughts of "no," "can't," or "won't" into "HOW," no matter how frustrating this might feel at first.
- Take time to explore options and continuously consider the deal from their perspective.

- Use "positive energy" rather than "defensive energy" to explore options.
- Make use of the planning tools in Chapter 9 to help visualize possible or different relationships between the issues.
- Ask the question: "Under what circumstances could we bridge the difference?"

KEY TAKEAWAYS

The fourteen behaviors offer a framework for The Complete Skilled Negotiator to develop and perform across all types of negotiations effectively. The more conscious you become at using these skills, where appropriate, the more likely you are to optimize your negotiation opportunities.

- Understand the behaviors you need to employ to perform at your best. Different stages of the negotiation will require the use of different behaviors.
- Work out what your behavioral strengths are and compensate for those which do not come naturally.
- Planning and preparation (7) is the most important activity you will undertake so don't "wing it."
- Behaviors help you to understand how to perform but do not help you with the "why." Be clear in your mind what you are trying to achieve and the various ways of arriving there.
- Disciplined behaviors alone will not make you an effective negotiator. You need to understand patience, nerve, power, and time before you can truly excel.
- Think as if you were inside their head – behave as an objective, conscious, competent negotiator.
- Comment on the link at the back of the book allowing the reader to profile themselves against the 14 behaviors and attract personal development recommendations.

CHAPTER 6

The "E" Factor

*"During a negotiation, it would be wise not to take anything personally.
If you leave personalities out of it, you will be able to see opportunities
more objectively."*

Brian Koslow

THE EFFECT OF HUMAN EMOTION ON NEGOTIATION

"How difficult can negotiation be? It's not rocket science." No, it is not. I would argue that it is more complex because it involves the most unpredictable of entities: human beings. Emotion makes negotiation highly unpredictable. The impact that this has on the dynamics found in negotiation is what I've defined as the "E" factor. Negotiators who are less self-aware struggle to control their emotions and, as a result, become readable and transparent to other negotiators. The more balanced, controlled, clearer thinkers use the "E" factor to their advantage, like seasoned poker players. The Complete Skilled Negotiator develops an eye for watching your every action and reaction as they gauge what is really going on inside your head.

Experienced negotiators:

- are conscious of what they are looking for;
- are calm in their thought process;
- are aware of the sensitivities in play; and
- send you the messages they *want* you to read.

Because every action attracts a reaction, trained negotiators work as hard at calculating how you will react to certain actions, and which signal to send that will most likely influence you during your negotiations.

No matter how many tactics, strategies, or variables are in play, it is people who make the decisions and it is people you need to understand; in particular, how you both behave in the heat of the moment. Unlike an engine, which is mechanically predictable and responds each and every time to the push of a throttle, negotiation and, importantly, people are less predictable.

Negotiation requires an attitude of mind based on self-discipline and self-control of emotion. What makes good negotiators into Complete Skilled Negotiators is that they not only execute negotiations using skills, tactics, and strategies but also recognize the attitudes and emotions, hidden or otherwise, that play a part in shaping the outcomes. It is emotional control, that allows for clear decision making. Behavioral control, mental control and emotional detachment are all needed to get inside the other party's head. You can never assume the reaction you are going to attract when tabling a proposal, especially when it's not one they are expecting. So the "E" in "E factor" is, you guessed it, for *emotion*. It is a conscious state that allows you to manage, use, manipulate, understand, and control it.

Many negotiation decisions in business are still emotionally influenced, even during sizeable complex deals. I'm not suggesting that deals take place without careful diligence or clear criteria and analysis. What I am suggesting from observation is that during negotiations, proposals and considerations are not always dealt with in the objective manner you might expect. Emotion and ego, as well as enterprise, have a significant role in influencing how decisions are taken.

The role of emotion

Emotion has its place when used in a considered and controlled manner:

- when the risks have been considered (walk out, outburst, deadlock);
- when its purpose is to attract a desired reaction; and

• when the seriousness of the issue needs conveying and you are confident that you will not ruin the chances of progress.

There is nothing wrong with a display of emotion during a negotiation, provided it is designed for effect and premeditated. The outburst in the middle of the meeting with a threat to walk away from the deal may appear irrational and hot-headed, but if the action were premeditated and the drama designed to attract a back-down from the other party, the emotional display can serve a useful purpose. This level of risk needs, however, to be a thought-through decision and one that is designed to attract a calculated response in an orchestrated manner. The real risks arise when we allow our decision making to be dictated by our own emotions and we start to react to their demands without thinking.

Understanding our emotions

Essentially, the emotion experienced by many in negotiation comes from uncertainty, risk, desire, and even fear: emotions that we have lived with for millions of years. But today we experience the types of dangers and risks that trigger these emotions less frequently than our ancestors and, more often than not, in a psychological context rather than in the physical form. As a result, we are less practiced and equipped to cope, meaning that even low levels of uncertainty for some can feel quite uncomfortable. For any emotionally driven negotiator this can lead to inappropriate decision making and sub-optimized deals, which is why an understanding of these emotions is important as part of your make-up as a negotiator.

The emotions of fear, hope, anger, envy, and greed resonate in us as strongly today as they ever have. Today there are ever more psychological models available to help us define what drives emotion, how people cope with it, and the effect that it will have on you. Yet, when faced with confrontation over a price increase in a negotiation, are we any more able to cope with what this does to our thinking and ability to perform? The answer is: only through greater levels of self-awareness and control.

Negotiation is uncomfortable and, when negotiating on behalf of your business, you are effectively being paid to be uncomfortable. If you concede unnecessarily or capitulate on a deal, you are not delivering on behalf of your employer.

THE TELL-TALE SIGNS OF STRESS

The pressure and stress that you experience in negotiation, however mild, are difficult to suppress and have their way of showing themselves through your physical actions. The stress you experience when tabling or rejecting proposals can start to exhibit itself through your body language. The act of touching your face, scratching your nose, brushing your hands through your hair, tapping your pen, folding your arms, or tapping your feet when making a proposal are all behavior changes, and will be seen by the other party who will be watching for them. You may not even be aware of it. Most are not. However, the other person will be watching every move you make. Whether they mean anything or not is unimportant. For now you need to understand that the other party are watching.

Effective negotiators learn to adapt to becoming more comfortable with being uncomfortable. This is achieved through heightened levels of self-awareness and becoming experienced in doing what is necessary from an objective standpoint, rather than allowing themselves to be victims of their emotion.

If you witness negotiators exhibiting these fidgety types of behaviors it may well mean nothing, other than an adjustment of their position. Reading body language, tends only to be relevant when change, speed, or the timing of movement correlates with something that has happened. If the other party responds to your proposal immediately, insisting that they will not or cannot accept the offer, observe their physical behavior as they respond. It is likely there will be some emotion involved. It is possible they mean it but it is also possible that they don't. Look for a correlation in body language or facial expressions if there is more than one of them negotiating. This is usually most recognizable when they are stating a position, rejecting a position, or making a statement.

- Listen to what they are saying, the way they are saying it, and what they do not say.
- Listen to whether they justify what they are saying.
- Listen to whether they go on to sell what they have just said.

The Complete Skilled Negotiator will see, hear, read, and interpret the meaning behind this as part of getting inside the other party's head.

If you, or those who negotiate on your behalf, experience high levels of anxiety, the resulting agreements are more likely to be compromised. The stress and anxiety of the process can lead you to concede or conclude agreements too early. Negotiating effectively requires nerve, as well as a mindset, which recognizes that it is not personal, it is business. Negotiators I have worked with who appear at least to have high levels of emotional control will and can mentally separate the people they negotiate with from the business of working on the deal.

WHEN THERE IS A NEED FOR A COLLABORATIVE SOLUTION

Part way through a negotiation involving the fees, specification, and time scales of an outsourced technology solution, the procurement team became frustrated at a lack of certainty, clarity, and absolute commitment to time scales. The "AGILE" system for managing the project offered the supplier more flexibility and less accountability to finish within the agreed specific time scales. The procurement team decided to impose penalty clauses in the event that the solution was not operational within 6 months. The clauses highlighted the importance of the time scales,

(Continued)

(Continued)

transferred some of the implications of non-delivery, and promoted a more formal relationship.

Meanwhile an internal agreement was being crafted between the finance and IT function of the same business. This, however, was an internal negotiation. A project involving the configuration of an online analytical tool used to measure sales conversion rates throughout the sales cycle was behind schedule. The program manager responsible remained evasive around the project completion dates. The CFO, under pressure from the board to provide more accurate forecasting, explained again the importance of the functionality to the business. The CFO could not directly introduce penalty clauses yet needed greater certainty. He was an internal client. He needed a long-term collaborative relationship with his colleagues in technology, so he engaged in a meeting to better understand their short-term challenges. He approached the issues from the perspective of how and under what circumstances the deadlines might be met in a problem-solving manner. Ultimately the CFO negotiated with marketing, asking them to agree to a 4-week slippage on their website project (releasing the same programmers as needed for his project) for a relaxation on their budget phasing, which he knew was under severe pressure. He presented the new window of opportunity to technology, who agreed to meet his more tightly defined time scales.

In the first example, the supplier was expected to take responsibility and be held accountable with commercial implications. In the second example, the attitude adopted was to work with those involved to question, listen, understand, and then propose solutions that helped to get the collaborative result needed. He had relationships to preserve so he adopted a collaborative, problem-solving stance.

CONSCIOUS COMPETENT

Any negotiator must become conscious of their own incompetencies before the developing the new skills or learning can begin. As you become more aware of specific negotiation skills and the effect they have on output you will also grow a greater awareness of your own development opportunities. The following model relates to four psychological states involved in progressing from incompetence to competence in a skill. The key to becoming more effective as a negotiator is to become a "conscious competent," by being able to consciously and competently to perform a skill or ability.

The advanced state of "unconscious competence" has its own handicap in that you tend to assume too much based on previous experience. So remaining in the conscious competent state for the purpose of negotiating is highly appropriate. Never assume anything in negotiation.

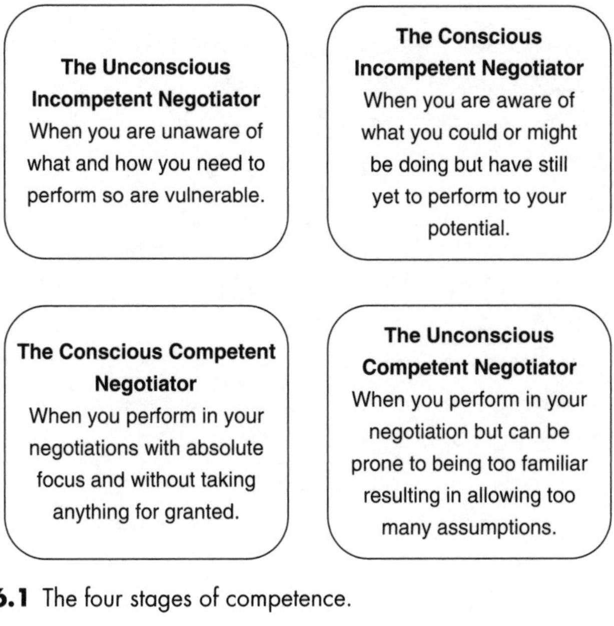

The Unconscious Incompetent Negotiator
When you are unaware of what and how you need to perform so are vulnerable.

The Conscious Incompetent Negotiator
When you are aware of what you could or might be doing but have still yet to perform to your potential.

The Conscious Competent Negotiator
When you perform in your negotiations with absolute focus and without taking anything for granted.

The Unconscious Competent Negotiator
When you perform in your negotiation but can be prone to being too familiar resulting in allowing too many assumptions.

Figure 6.1 The four stages of competence.

BROKEN RECORD

During a negotiation for storage facilities with a port management company in Amsterdam, we were close to agreeing on a 3-year extension to an existing contract that had 6 months remaining to run. It had taken as many months to reach this point and, although dialog had been constructive throughout, I concluded that their COO was either not able or not prepared to move on the fixed monthly payment schedule regardless of activity volume. They wanted to charge the average monthly invoice value from the past 30 months. Our volumes arriving at port were volatile and not represented by averages. We tried introducing other negotiation variables, but he would not budge and just continued to insist, like a broken record, "you will need to agree to the monthly fixed charge." He then started to become emotional saying that everything was possible (although we had learned earlier that this wasn't the case) but we must move to the monthly fixed cost.

We had tried quarterly adjustments, offered $100,000 on account to cover any variance, but he wanted us to sign this monthly fixed charge, which eventually we did. Commercially it was not an issue and the deal had to be done. The truth is that he had worn us down and we had not realistic options. For 3 hours it's all we heard. The repeated position, like a broken record, gained more credibility as a given, the more it was stated. On reflection, there were many other ways that he might have got my signature quicker. However, we concluded that the prospect of extended discussions with an ever more emotional partner was not worth any possible benefit that I might derive from further perseverance. Like most tactics used in negotiation, they are not right or wrong and may suit some relationships and not others. The choice and consequences remain for you to judge.

BECOMING A CONSCIOUSLY COMPETENT NEGOTIATOR THROUGH UNDERSTANDING TA

Back in the 1950s, Dr Eric Berne defined the ego states known to us today as transactional analysis (TA). In the book *I'm OK, You're OK*, the author Thomas Harris analyzed Berne's work, which was made up of definitions of ego states and how they affect the way we communicate with each other. These are defined as the roles of:

- parent (critical and nurturing);
- adult; and
- child (free and adaptive).

These are communication styles that we all use subconsciously whilst communicating with others. Within negotiation, these ego states resonate in the language and behavior used, which can directly impact on expectations, respect, irrationality, arrogance, and other attitudes exercised during discussions.

The "parent" ego state

The "parent" ego state is made up of two ego states: the "critical parent" and the "nurturing parent."

The language of the critical parent's ego state is "black and white" or "right and wrong" with very few shades of grey, suggesting that they are in a position to make the rules, judge, and criticize others. However, what is important in your negotiations is that you do not allow such communication to affect the way you read the situation.

In negotiation, some people have been known to use this stance to take control. It can be a difficult force to reason with when they

(Continued)

(Continued)

remain inflexible and stubborn, especially when they are negotiating from a position of power. They will know it and will use it, sometimes naturally and sometimes orchestrated, but always aimed at controlling your aspirations.

The "nurturing parent," on the other hand, wants to advise and guide. They want respect and want to be needed. They want to protect, so any "child" showing respect and asking for help is likely to attract a positive response from a nurturing parent. However, they are also at risk of becoming manipulated by those communicating as a "child."

The "child" ego state

The "child" ego state is also made up of two ego states: the "free child" and the "adapted child."

The "free child" is spontaneous, creative, and fun loving in their attitude and communication, whereas the "adapted child" is rebellious, non-compliant and manipulative ("It's not fair," "See what you've made me do").

The "child" commonly shirks responsibility, is sometimes manipulative, sometimes subservient, but is always a product of those around them. These behaviors, thoughts, and feelings are replayed from our own childhood and, depending on our circumstances, will feature in how we communicate throughout our lives. This can result in our feeling victimized by the rules that others lay down, or underpin our desire to challenge authority.

Responses to ego states

In negotiation, behaving in the "parent" ego state can result in others adopting the behavioral response of a "child" ego state. Where you find yourself negotiating with a "critical parent" character, you may choose instead to appeal to their nurturing parent instinct. Two "parents" clashing is simply two egos vying for control and domination, which will frequently lead to impasse, and the break-down of the relationship and any pending negotiations.

If you adopt the "child" ego state, you are of course effectively manipulating their ego by asking them how they might be able to help you, given your weaker position. There are risks to this, in that they may choose to manipulate the situation even further. However, once the "parent" recognizes that there is no fight to be had, and that you are asking for help, their nurturing ego is triggered and they generally become far more accommodating.

The "adult" ego state

When in our "adult" ego state, we are more able to see people and situations as they are, rather than being intimidated or manipulative. We are more likely to make decisions based on a pragmatic, objective analysis of any given situation, rather than be swayed by the emotional ego that exists in the "child" or "parent" states. If there was a preferred default position from which to negotiate, it would be the "adult" ego state.

Listen and watch out for the behavior of the "black and white," "right and wrong" dominant "parent."

Listen and watch out for the positioning of the "child," who seeks to seduce you, or make irrational demands, in that they need your help and appeal to your sense of parenting.

The "adult," on the other hand, is objective in thought, can accommodate many shades of grey, can recognize irrational behavior, and sees most types of behavior and language for what they are. They generally operate as conscious competent negotiators.

Clearly, though, this is only an ego state and even "adults" can still be quickly influenced into moving to other ego states during negotiations. Imagine you were challenged on your opening position by a "parent," who tells you how ridiculous you are being, and not to come back until

(Continued)

(*Continued*)

you are prepared to be sensible. The decision here is whether to respond as a "critical parent" and challenge them – with the risk of intensifying the conflict – or adopt the ego state of the "free child" and ask them for help. If you are not sure, you may choose to maintain your composure as an "adult," dismiss their behavior, and wait patiently for them to calm down before continuing. As always, it depends on the circumstances. What is important is that we recognize these states in others as well as ourselves and that we adapt accordingly, rather than continue, oblivious to the emotion influencing the dynamics of the relationship and communication.

The "E" factor can make or break a deal, or the longer-term prospects of a relationship. This makes self-awareness an important part of the Complete Skilled Negotiator's make-up. Those who are successful at negotiating in the long term are more likely to have "adult-to-adult" relationships, although in the real world irrational behavior is in no short supply.

YOUR VALUES

Your personal values and your business values are often very similar. They can be based on such qualities as integrity, honesty, reliability, and others. They provide you with the parameters to judge what you believe is fair, what behavior you find acceptable and the degree to which you are prepared to allow others to use the power they have during your dealings.

Your values may well provide you with a balance in how you lead your life, how you make decisions, interpret right from wrong, and so on. However, in negotiation, they can often serve to distort your thinking (see behavior 1, Chapter 5). Whether the behavior of the other party is ethical, "fair," or "right" is of little consequence in negotiation. If they have the power and decide to be irrational with it, it is your job to manage the situation as you find it. It is not the time to start making value judgments. Cling to your ideals and you will become emotionally challenged and compromised.

EMOTIONAL INTELLIGENCE

If there is one critical competency central to effective negotiation, I would suggest it is emotional intelligence. It underpins the balance of communication between you and those you negotiate with, and promotes the concept of negotiating from inside their head.

In his 1995 book, *Emotional Intelligence*, Daniel Goleman describes how emotional intelligence is made up of two parts. He claims that to be effective in business, you need to have a high level of self-awareness and self-control around your emotions and those of the other party:

- first, by understanding yourself, your intentions, your responses, and your own behavior;
- second, by understanding others and their feelings.

This is critical in negotiations because you are responsible for the feelings of those you negotiate with. Antagonize the other party and watch any hope of cooperation dissolve. Goleman goes on to describe the five "domains" of emotional intelligence:

1. Knowing our emotions.
2. Managing your own emotions.
3. Motivating yourself.
4. Recognizing and understanding other people's emotions.
5. Managing relationships and the emotions of others.

Extroverts, who tend to be more communicative, tend to be more openly emotional people. They are more inclined to share and articulate their views, likes, and dislikes. However, extroverts are faced with a greater challenge because the control required during a negotiation involves a greater level of self-discipline than it does with introverts, who are naturally more considered in their responses.

Introverts are more inclined to reflect, weigh, and consider before responding.

Imagine watching a film that involves two parties negotiating. The actors are engaged in a negotiation, and one of them is performing so poorly that it starts to make you cringe. "Why did they say that?", "You've just given away your position by saying that," "I would never have responded in that way," you might think to yourself.

During negotiation workshops at The Gap Partnership, we often provide challenging case study exercises for individuals and groups to negotiate with each other. The negotiations are recorded on video to help the attendees observe and learn about the appropriateness of their behavior given their objectives. We help them to analyze their planning, behavior, self-control, and performance. Today we work with hundreds of case studies from our library, which are each designed to focus on different learning outcomes in different industries, working with different groups of negotiating variables. There are some multi-issue case studies which so accurately lead to predictable behavior that I have used them time after time. You could predict, minutes before an attendee negotiating did something, what they were going to do. The coaching that follows is based around the appropriateness of their motives, emotions, and decision making, which provides a powerful lesson in self-awareness every time.

But what was it that made their actions so predictable? Competitiveness? Pride? The need to perform? A desire to use the skills we had already covered to positive effect? It was their ego and the competitive situation that led to a narrowing of the mind, the capacity to think, weigh and consider. It becomes personal, despite the considerable commercial experience and background of those I have worked with. It has driven individuals (thousands over the years) to justify their often short-term irrational behavior because of the pressure they felt resulting from the circumstances they had been placed in. They were willing, under certain circumstances, to compete, even though their brief was to focus on the total value opportunity.

Negotiating agreements successfully in business can be very challenging in that commercial pressures combined with an obligation to deliver will naturally stimulate competitiveness. Business is all about "winning" and outperforming competitors. However, your competitor is not the person you are negotiating with. From the many organizations where I have spent time facilitating negotiations, I have concluded that the bigger the desire to "win," the greater the chance of distorted thinking during negotiations and the less emotional intelligence used. Resist the temptation to allow your ego to color your judgment. Winning in negotiation means building successful agreements that the other party will deliver against. It is about building value and enhancing the bottom line. In some cases it might be about gaining a commitment to change that minimizes disruption, or simply reducing the risks associated with an existing arrangement. What it is not about is you, or whether you have won. If you allow this thought or feeling to dominate your motivation your performance will most likely be compromised.

THE ART OF LOSING

Negotiation is about the art of losing, or the art of letting others have *your* way. With your ego out of the way, and your attitude firmly focused on the outcome of the agreement, you are free to behave in any way you believe to be appropriate to your interests. Being what you need to be and doing what you need to do includes allowing the other party to enjoy the "symbols of success" whilst you focus on the total value of the agreement. This means understanding others and their needs and then trading off no more than you need to in order to optimize your net position. It means letting them win on items of less significance whilst you focus on the more significant, value-adding variables. You could argue that you cannot afford to set precedents by allowing them to win the psychological battle even on some issues (depending on whether there is an ongoing trading relationship or not), or that if you concede on certain issues they will expect this in the future. However, your job as a negotiator is also to help the other party to feel as though they have won.

In situations like this when you feel as though you are losing control of the relationship, emotions can take over and your decision-making capacity can become compromised. Your position and scope to negotiate also become compromised by circumstances and the proactivity being employed by your prospective customer. Your immediate reaction may be, "this is not fair, not right, and I'm not even sure I want to work with them anymore," which runs counter to your business interests. Despite your reactive stance, now is the time to consider your response and advise them of your position. Develop your strategy and do not react emotionally. There are two options for preventing this type of situation *before you even start to negotiate*.

1. Always establish whether there is a buying process involved that you should be aware of.
2. Always identify the decision maker(s) and any other stakeholders who are involved in the sign-off of agreements.

MANAGING THE EMOTIONAL NEED FOR SATISFACTION

We touched briefly on the need for satisfaction in Chapter 1. The need that individuals have for "satisfaction" – meaning getting a better deal than what was originally available – can be so strong that many negotiators use relative positioning and inflexibility at the start of a negotiation with the aim of letting the other party achieve what they thought at the beginning of discussions to be difficult if not impossible. Open your tough negotiations at a position you know they will reject and it is the start of the process of "give and take," which will allow you to start managing the other party's need for satisfaction. Many inexperienced negotiators start with a figure that they know the other party can accept because of the fear of hearing the word "no."

Get used to the word "no." When you open with a position that is extreme and yet realistic, you are going to hear it a lot. It is part of the process and you should expect it. Keep the dialogue open and they are less likely to walk away. If they tell you they can't or won't agree to your opening offer, invite them to tell you how close they can get to your offer. It keeps the dialogue going and it gets them to talk about your position. Rather than allowing them to get emotional, ask them what they would agree to rather than what they will not agree to. Then stop and consider your next move.

One of the benefits of opening first in negotiation is that you create an anchor, a position to move from and a position for them to attack. This should be on the right side of where you expect to finish up, rather than reacting to their position and playing in their "ball park." Be proactive and open first. Take the rejection and then move forward. You are managing their satisfaction and at the same time you are involved in the process of securing the best possible deal. It provides you with the opportunity to maximize the deal whilst still allowing them to take emotional satisfaction even though they may be finishing on their own break point.

THE NEED TO MANAGE SATISFACTION

Ivan Chen is the general manager at Hong Kong-based paint company White and White, who specialize in eco-friendly lime wash paints with an "unmatched color range." Following an article in a Condé Nast magazine, White and White benefited from a fourfold surge in overseas orders, which was sustained for 6 consecutive months. Following this unsolicited success, White and White decided to engage in an advertising campaign via the Condé Nast group.

Six full pages, one each month for 6 months, was the plan. Their rate card price per page advert was $35,000 for global coverage (31 publications) plus charges for an online presence, called the dual package.

Following several calls and emails with their VP of advertising, Ivan offered $154,000 for the six slots. He responded with a copy of the rate card stating that the fee was $270,000 for the dual package, minus a 15% discount for six slots. The price at the bottom of the email was a daunting $229,500 but Ivan ignored "the power of the written

(Continued)

(*Continued*)

word." He agreed to meet a week later offering them time to think about it. He was authorized to go up to $200,000 for the six slots.

In the second meeting he felt he was not making progress so he adjourned and arranged a third meeting with the VP and also Gary Chow, the President of Marketing, at their offices in Causeway Bay. During this final 2-hour meeting, Gary offered additional extras including video-based advertising footage for mobiles and tablets, and enhanced in-magazine positioning, in an attempt to close the deal. Ivan increased his offer to £174,000, subject to artwork support for the adverts and additional mentions in the opening address from the Editor.

At 6.30pm and with pressure mounting, Gary introduced the idea of an additional advertorial at no extra cost – a half-page article presented by White & White independently and yet favorably. Ivan made his final move. "If you agree to £188,500 per six-slot campaign, I will agree to run two campaigns over 24 months at one slot every other month. That's 12 slots in total subject to us maintaining our current enquiry levels, otherwise I can execute an opt-out clause after the first six slots." Ivan had increased volume, managed risk, and provided price satisfaction in his move. Gary took the deal.

Ivan might have offered the full $200,000, but understood that this was a limit and not a target. He was satisfied that the extra concessions agreed were good value and had been authorized to increase the scope of the offer to 12 slots. The satisfaction of both parties and the commitment to the deal came from the many hours it took to finally agree. It felt worth having. The harder you work on a deal, the more challenging it is to complete, and so commitments are more likely to be honored. Conversely, if it's too good to be true, and the deal is wrapped up too quickly, it shouldn't surprise you how many of these agreements fall apart as quickly as they come together.

THE "E" FACTOR   117

Banks and real-estate agents are known for trying to manage satisfaction, but often the individuals responsible for the negotiations simply don't have the nerve to carry through the transaction in a controlled manner. Take the estate agent who tells you: "Our fee is 1.75% of the selling price, but we know it's a competitive market ... so we are prepared to do it for 1.5%." Did I get any satisfaction from this move? No. It was quick, unconditional, and transparent. They didn't even wait for a response, or find out whether I have already been offered 1.5% elsewhere, or establish that I wanted to work with them anyway because of their great service levels, for example. The bank manager who states: "We are currently offering our business clients an overdraft facility of base plus 4%. However, in your case we are prepared to offer base plus 3.5%."

Why? So that I feel better? I did not have to work for it or even meet a condition. It wasn't even a deciding factor at the time, so why offer it? Satisfaction comes from having to work for it. Even those in the crowds at the sales have to hunt down the deals in the high street, investing hours of time to get the 25% off deal. They may not have negotiated, but they have invested their time and effort. Those involved in the process will feel satisfied with their bargain.

If someone agrees too easily, you have a decision and commitment that can just as easily be reversed. Psychologically, things that are hard to attain carry a greater value. Deals that have been hard fought for are more likely to be honored. Regard the process of working towards agreement as an investment in the agreement's sustainability or the likelihood of it being honored.

Remember that you can get a great price but a lousy deal if the other party do not deliver on their commitments as has been agreed. For example, if it does not arrive on time, or if it doesn't do the job you need it for, the price makes up only one part of the overall equation.

Working within fixed budgets can mean that your budget is finite. When restricted in this way, it is important to understand the effect this may have on what you agree regarding specification. Will the product or service be de-specified to allow for the price? Is this clear up-front or is it likely to come to light only once the agreement has been made? Maintaining focus and discipline throughout your negotiation means ensuring you are thorough when it comes to covering all the issues, risks, specification, timing, and any other factors that could result in you receiving less than what you believe you had agreed to. Unfortunately, those who remain in denial use budget constraints as an excuse for poor deals that often fail to deliver.

TRUST, TACTICS, AND EMOTIONS

The trust and respect that you build in your relationships allow for discussion and the opportunity to build agreements. Your energy can then be spent on the deal rather than on positioning and managing the emotional needs of those involved. Between 9 o'clock and 12 o'clock this relationship state provides the ideal place to maximize value. Some negotiators say they want to work in a partnership and yet behave tactically back around at 6 o'clock. They may even start to introduce demands that they don't even want. Why? Because they are still attempting to provide you with the satisfaction of negotiating the demands off the table.

Like most tactics, this can be transparent and can prove detrimental to your interests, especially if you need to maintain trust and integrity for the relationship to work. It can also result in the discussions being emotionally charged and most likely result in transactional agreements yielding less value.

TRUST IS VALUABLE AND YET FRAGILE

John Whitehouse, an Australian boxing promoter, presented the manager for middle-weight boxer Wayne Greenwood with a contract that featured 37 clauses. Wayne's manager as usual handed the contract over to his lawyers.

They identified three unusual clauses that had not featured or ever been mentioned before. They were linked to levels of indemnity insurance, restrictions on pre- and post-fight interviews, and the rights to promote the fighter in his next three fights if he won.

Facing the risk of contract discussions breaking down, Wayne's lawyers re-wrote the contract and presented it as an agenda along with a condition of continued discussions. Despite John Whitehouse's insistence that he works in partnership with managers and agents, discussions became more formal and guarded. The new contract still included the three original clauses, but had been adapted, along with a further three new clauses aimed at protecting Wayne's future options.

The promoter soon realized that not only were the lawyers prepared, but he was now going to have to work harder within a transactional relationship to make headway on the remaining clauses. He had introduced the additional clauses to effectively trade away during discussions but in doing so had reduced any trust that may have existed.

VISIBLE EMOTION

Visible emotion is sometimes used tactically in negotiation. One such tactic known as the "professional flinch" (see Chapters 5 and 8) involves one party making their opening proposal and the other reacting with an exaggerated emotional reaction, implying that the offer is ridiculous. The emotion, orchestrated, is designed to provide a far more powerful form of rejection than a simple "no." As a negotiator you need to read the situation and be confident of your actions. There is no place for uncontrolled emotion in negotiation. As a Complete Skilled Negotiator, you need to be in control of your thinking, reactions, what you say, and what you decide not to say.

Another way of deliberately controlling visible emotions is when negotiators make power statements during the opening exchanges of a discussion as part of anchoring the aspirations of the other party. As they do so, they are consciously waiting for the reactions to gauge how far they might push a particular issue. For example: "We're pleased we've been able to get together to discuss some of the issues around our compensation claim today," or "Clearly you recognize that this is most unusual and that any settlement is likely to take months if not years to conclude given the complexity of the issue." The anchor statement may have no substance at all. The person making the statement is watching and listening for the emotional signals that suggest rejection or acceptance of the statement. The Complete Skilled Negotiator would counter with an alternative statement. This effectively reverses the power statement back to the other party.

Emotion, pressure, and stress are commonplace in negotiation. With the implications of deadlock, the responsibility to deliver, and the frustration that can come with working through agreements, self-control often gives way to our subconscious. You start to do things you are not even aware of. Most people I have worked with do not believe this until they see it for themselves on video, but non-verbal communication becomes exaggerated during stressful times, especially when statements or threats are being made.

Telling the other party what you *will* do at any given point in your discussions (even if it's not the best offer you could make) is a useful discipline for getting them to focus on your position. You have to accommodate patience and frustration whilst options are considered. Sometimes the other party themselves may start to show signs of emotion or stress. Usually this is most evident when responding to or making a proposal.

Imagine you know that you can agree at $1000, but have opened your position at $600. They ask you: "Is that your best price?", to which you reply, "That's the price I am prepared to pay." They then make you an offer of $1100. You say: "I can move to $725 but that will need to include the service agreement and delivery by Monday." All the time you are seeking to trade price against other value items but, in the back of your mind, you know that you can go further and would be prepared to do so if the alternative was to lose the deal, which even at $1000 is as good as your best alternative. They pause, having heard you say $725, and there is a moment of silence. Are they thinking about it, preparing to walk away or considering their next move? The 20 seconds that have passed feel like 5 minutes.

Their silence may be suggesting to you that your offer is ridiculous and that they have no interest in further conversations. The fact that they are still in discussions is a non-verbal suggestion that there is some level of interest. The Complete Skilled Negotiator understands that nothing happens by accident in negotiation. Everything, every movement, statement, response, and moment of silence happens for a reason, so you will maintain composure, will watch, and will listen.

Your job as a negotiator is to read and interpret the correlation between what is being *said* and *how* the other party is *behaving*.

During the experiential negotiation workshops I have provided the opportunity to negotiate agreements whilst being recorded on video, allowing for detailed analysis of everything that takes place. It allows negotiators to see for themselves the degree to which their actions and emotions are visible. Most people completely deny that they would give any type of signal away until they see themselves on camera. Once they have and accept this, it results in a significant leap in consciously controlled performances. Listen to what they say, watch what they do and then calculate your response.

Conscious negotiators are capable of active listening. This involves intentionally demonstrating to others that you are listening, engaged, and open-minded, if that's what you want them to think. In other words, they are skilled at providing the signals through their own body language that they want the other party to receive. Part of getting into the other party's head is getting them to think what you *want* them to think.

Emotional ego
How many times have you seen emotion or ego-fueled behavior at charity auctions, let alone business auctions? The entire event is geared to provide maximum personal exposure in the room. The compère walks around calling the bidders by their name: "now that's $5000 for the football shirt,

has Mr John Smith the nerve to increase his bid?" As he turns to Mr Smith, so does the attention of the audience. Of course Mr Smith has the nerve, and he doesn't want to lose face. These businessmen at the auctions who are clearly successful, and who have probably worked very hard for such sums, regard this as a fun process. They are seduced by the immediate public recognition for their generosity and dismiss the very judgment they usually exercise that probably helped them make the money in the first place. It's for charity. It is their money (although not always), so I can understand their "fun." However, on many occasions similar actions have been witnessed in the business world where the egos of those involved use "company money," fueled by the need to win, and exercise disregard for the very shareholders they are working on behalf of.

Emotion distorts objectivity. If your spouse was being held captive and a ransom was being demanded for their release, the last person who should negotiate the agreement is you. You are emotionally involved and therefore immediately compromised. You would probably give everything you own for their release, probably in your first offer, assuming the kidnappers had not already stated their demand. You should of course delegate the role of negotiating to another person. They may be no more competent than you at negotiating, but they will be without the emotional attachment that you have to the outcome.

KEY TAKEAWAYS

Careful planning ahead of your negotiation may help your confidence and provide you with considered options. However, emotional behavior and the actions of the other party, together with circumstantial changes, require nerve, self-awareness, and self-control, otherwise your composure and performance may be compromised.

- Understand yourself, your intentions, your responses, your emotions, and your own behavior.
- Try to understand the deal from inside the other party's head and the priorities, interests, pressures, and emotions they will be feeling.

- Listen, understand, calculate, think, and slow down. It will increase your mental capacity and will make a real difference to your performance.
- Even where strong dependent relationships exist, with pressure and tension, emotion is never far away.
- Planning and preparation, starting with an agenda, will help you promote order, options, and more collaborative dialog.
- When unclear, feeling under pressure, or without the clarity you feel you need, take time out – otherwise you may find yourself facing the unintended consequences of your rash actions.
- Don't be seduced by large concessions. Their extreme opening position may well have been designed to shock and then satisfy you.
- Keep your ego in check. Only then are you free to behave in any way you believe to be appropriate to your interests.
- Never take for granted how others may behave. Human beings under pressure can become irrational in thinking and in their behavior.

CHAPTER 7

Authority and Empowerment

"No one should be without accountability. It is a dangerous and lonely place to be."

Unknown

UNDERSTANDING EMPOWERMENT

Your negotiations can only progress if communication flows and those who are directly or indirectly involved are allowed to take decisions. Therefore, understanding the role of empowerment in your negotiation is fundamental to managing the relationships and communications that stand between you and progress.

However, with empowerment comes exposure and this brings with it risk. It is this risk that organizations seek to control by empowering individuals with limits, or caps, beyond which they must escalate to higher authority. Too much empowerment and any individual can become dangerous or vulnerable and therefore so can the organization they work for.

The Complete Skilled Negotiator will understand empowerment in terms of:

- how it can be used to protect you;
- how it affects your ability to be creative;
- how it affects your ability to build value; and
- how it affects the other party's thinking and behavior.

Essentially, it is the degree to which you can negotiate and take decisions without having to refer or escalate them to a higher authority. In other words, empowerment relates to the scope and range of variables and the authority within which you have to negotiate or operate. If you regard empowerment as simply a gauge to broaden or narrow your trading opportunities, or to provide "stop limits" up to which you can negotiate, you can start to get a feel for how empowerment can work for you, as well as against you.

To negotiate collaboratively on the left-hand side of the clock face (6–12 o'clock) requires the scope or empowerment to work with many variables and possibilities. Limiting this, as many organizations do, can help protect you from the escalation and disempowerment tactics sometimes used by others. So getting this right is fundamental to where you will finish up on the clock face.

Great negotiators tend to be unsung heroes. Great deals become so over time as the contract delivers the value it was intended to offer, rather than necessarily at the time when the deal was completed. Negotiators often work as part of a team, which can involve specialist lawyers, finance directors, and others. Because the last person to become involved in the negotiation dealings is the boss, the act of negotiation is usually and appropriately delegated further down the line, further diluting the transparency of who is actually controlling events. And when the deal is done, the need for confidentiality as well as the need to protect the operations of those companies involved means that the true facts and figures agreed are rarely publicized to the degree to which you can measure the relative performance of the negotiators involved.

Most high-profile negotiators tend to be political figures or union leaders, because they use PR as part of posturing during or leading up to discussions. However, these individuals neither work by themselves nor are they fully empowered to negotiate on all issues. Using the press and media is part of how they frame, anchor, and publicize their position and progress to those they represent, the parties they are negotiating with, and any other third parties.

One of my personal experiences as a negotiator involved facilitating a highly-charged negotiation between a Japanese electronics company and a trade union in the UK. The level of trust between the parties involved, together with the climate of the meeting and the relationship, was poor, hence the need to bring in a neutral to facilitate events. On my advice to my client, I was provided with no scope with which to negotiate, which allowed me to focus on the process and not be drawn on specific proposals. My role included helping the parties with establishing solutions, starting with why they thought they could not agree to the terms that had already been tabled.

How empowered are they?

Rushing into negotiations without qualifying whether the other party is empowered to negotiate is a mistake many eager and ultimately frustrated account managers have made. The need to question, qualify, and explore requires patience. It is during this phase of initial discussions that the issue of empowerment should be qualified by simply asking: "Are you in a position to sign off the agreement?" or "Who else would you need to consult with as part of signing off this agreement?" or even "What limits are there that might prevent you from signing off the agreement?" All of these questions will help you to decide whether you are dealing with the right person or people.

Being disempowered

We are socially conditioned to conform and most of us lead our lives respecting the laws of where we live and others around us. Laws provide in some instances freedom of movement, for example, effectively empowering us to travel and choose how and where we travel. Laws can also disempower us, in that we may not travel faster than a given speed or, when driving, having drunk alcohol, and so on.

The written word carries an assumed authority in that it has been published. It is designed to be legitimate. In your negotiation the other party may present you with, say, a price list. Rather than accepting this as it is, you should regard it as their opening position. Different situations require different considerations, yet many will wrongly assume that not only is the printed price fixed but the person issuing it is disempowered to negotiate.

The more empowered you are, however, the more exposed you become. You may carry more risk to your business and therefore be accountable for the total impact of your actions. Organizations have a tough challenge in providing a level of empowerment to their employees which helps the business conduct "good business" but not with such risks that the "good business" could be concluded with unintended consequences or unforeseen costs.

Many organizations actively promote business values such as creativity, entrepreneurship, and even empowerment. Yet when negotiating with suppliers and customers they recognize that there have to be limits within which individuals are empowered to operate, otherwise the business will lose total control of its operation. They operate a disempowered structure to protect their own business operation.

For example, they might use a price list, which serves to disempower the salesperson, as does the accompanying printed discount structure. Under these circumstances, the salesperson is disempowered to the point where they are little more than an order taker.

If the customer demands better terms they have to speak to the boss. The boss, a supervisor, is also disempowered. They have a boss and if you can get to them, because they are usually "out of town," you may just be able to negotiate a better deal.

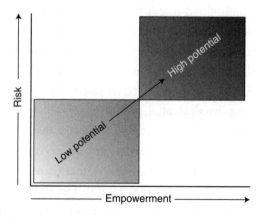

Figure 7.1 Empowerment.

Tactically, empowerment allows you to use a third party, citing your lack of authority to move further, which serves to deflect the pressure away from you. If not used carefully though, it can backfire.

Fully empowered individuals can become very dangerous
Rogue traders acting beyond their company's agreed levels of empowerment provide us with ample evidence of just how badly things can go wrong if scope, when provided, goes unchecked.

HISTORY'S LESSONS FROM THOSE WHO WERE "EMPOWERED"

Navinda Singh Sarao from the UK was charged in 2015 with ten counts of commodities fraud after manipulating the S&P 500 futures contracts, which resulted in it plunging by 600 points ($500bn) in a matter of minutes. The flash crash, which was said to have caused chaos across US equities, was a result of an automated trading program he used, placing multiple simultaneous large sell orders at different price points, a technique known as spoofing. He was said to have personally made $27m over 4 years.

The biggest fraud in history was carried out by Jerome Kerviel of Société Générale, who had taken up hedging positions that cost his business €4.9bn. At one point, he ran up about €38bn in unauthorized trades, which when discovered had to be carefully unwound. The bank almost collapsed as a result of the losses discovered in 2008.

Another notable example involving empowered City traders is that of Kweku Adoboli, who in 2011 lost UBS £1.4bn. He was described as being "a gamble or two away from destroying Switzerland's largest bank." He was jailed for 7 years after being found guilty of fraud.

(Continued)

(*Continued*)

At the center of the subprime mortgage scandal at Credit Suisse in London, David Higgs was found guilty of falsifying accounts in a New York court. As Managing Director of Credit Suisse in London in 2007 and 2008 he had inflated the value of mortgage securities in the bank's portfolio. The overstatement forced Credit Suisse to announce a $2.85bn (£1.8bn) write down.

These are just a few of the more well-publicized examples of what can happen when those who have been partially empowered operate outside the limits set, and without the necessary transparency and checks to protect everyone concerned.

Being partially empowered

Every industry uses empowerment limits to protect their business. Call centers use this to make it almost impossible for customers to negotiate with their representatives, who stick rigidly to their scripts. Any demand proposal made by the customer that sits outside the script has to be escalated to their supervisor – a classic avoidance strategy where the customer has to escalate or, if not, give up and concede. However where the discussion does deadlock and the customer cancels the order, supply or subscription you have to ask is it not better to provide the call center operator with some tools and skills to work with. Other examples include: the insurance industry with the salesperson who can only refer to the underwriter for a decision; the shop assistant who has to refer to their manager when challenged by a customer; and the hotel receptionist who has to check with their manager before agreeing to that special rate. Even the empowered negotiator may sometimes use the tactic of suggesting that their boss would not agree and therefore cannot agree to the offer on the table.

In life we are surrounded by limits and rules, for the most part set in place to protect us from ourselves. For instance, a police officer can stop you, arrest you, or take you into custody, but is not empowered to sentence you.

That is the role of a judge, who in turn is governed by the rule of law, the jury, and the evidence. This process serves to prevent corruption and protects the system, whichever side of it you may be on. Within the context of a job, in the case of the police, they have the authority, responsibility, and ultimately have been empowered to go so far in the apprehension process. What they can and can't do as part of apprehending a suspect has been clearly defined in their training. It provides them with the confidence to escalate issues that are outside of their remit in the same way that you should operate with pre-agreed parameters within which you have been authorized.

YOUR BOSS CAN BE YOUR WORST ENEMY

The most dangerous person in any organization is the person with the most authority – usually the boss. The person who can say "yes" and knows that they are able to do so is more likely to do so, and under pressure they often do. If you have ever attended a meeting alongside your boss you may well have experienced the following typical and yet frustrating scenario. It is *your* client relationship but your boss wants to sit in for whatever reason. The meeting starts and you set out to discuss some of the challenging issues with your client, and then your boss starts to take over the conversation. In no time at all, your client and boss are fully engaged in the discussion; they start exploring solutions and ultimately start trading concessions that you would not have been empowered to offer yourself. Your boss still thinks that they are doing the right thing and a great job at that.

What has happened, though, is that your boss is as keen as you are to resolve the issue. They are, however, more empowered (which, as we know, makes them more dangerous). Before long, your boss has concluded the meeting having built an agreement. Your boss has probably involved you along the way, yet may still have undermined your relationship and credibility with your client. Guess who the client asks to see at the next meeting?

Your boss may be highly skilled, have tremendous nerve and be very capable of managing relationships. However, they have a greater responsibility and accountability than you and therefore will be more exposed and will have more to lose if the deal deadlocks. As they are most empowered, hold the weakest negotiating position of anyone in your organization. Imagine your king in a game of chess. The king is not as mobile as the other pieces. If your king is in check, you will always be vulnerable no matter how many pieces you have on the board. Therefore, your job is to protect your king, to ensure that the other party does not gain access to them. In negotiation, your king is your boss and it is not in your interest to expose your boss directly to the other party, otherwise you could find yourself in a compromised position. There is a famous mantra preached by buyers: "another level, another percent." The buyer will negotiate hard with their counterpart and then try to escalate to the next level to get that extra percent concession, and then escalate again for another percent and so on.

Who is in the background?

So if you are ultimately accountable it is in your interests to disempower yourself as this will protect you. Better to manage in the background and let the discussions unfold, than to be the focus of attention. Make it known that others will be taking the decisions and that you will back whatever decisions are taken.

In any negotiation, never assume that you are dealing with the ultimate decision maker. You may find yourself being enlightened at the end of your discussions, that is, they have to refer the final decision to somebody else. The person you thought you were negotiating with was in fact not empowered to make the final decision. They may have also made offers that their business will not carry out. You may have even offered concessions in return for discount levels that the other person is ultimately not authorized to agree. Therefore, it's imperative always to qualify the degree to which the other person is empowered:

- establish who the decision maker is; and
- establish who else will need to agree.

Do this before the negotiation begins. If not, you will leave yourself wide open to tactics, stalling, escalation, or, worse still, agree to a contract that will not be delivered on, because the terms agreed were not viable.

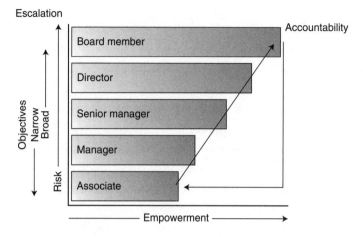

Figure 7.2 Escalation.

Gaining "in principle" agreements
Another way of using the boss to help negotiations flow where there is likely to be a high level of resistance is in arranging top-to-top meetings between senior management. These meetings are used to outline ideas and for gaining "in-principle" agreements, allowing for negotiations on the detail to follow up. This is used in both political and business environments as a means of protecting the boss from specific exposure, whilst allowing for trust and an understanding to be built between the two parties at a senior level.

MAKING USE OF HIGHER AUTHORITY

A local restauranteur Rob had secured a wealthy celebrity backer who was attracted by the opportunity to lease 15,000 square feet of space for a licensed restaurant opportunity at an established Tuscan Marina.

Over the previous 4 years, the Marina, which was in an excellent town location, had attracted strong competition. Pressure had built up on mooring rates and waiting lists had evaporated. The invest- ment in the quality of services expected by wealthy yacht owners

(Continued)

was simply being better met elsewhere. The Marina was privately owned by a group of local businessmen whose borrowing capacity had been exhausted, so was not in a position to borrow in order to invest further.

Having terminated the contract with the existing team running the Marina Café, they engaged in conversations with Rob, who maintained from the outset that he was only acting on behalf of his investor. The Marina management team's idea was to attract an investment to build and operate a "destination restaurant" that would attract not only boat owners but local residents.

As the final terms were due to be agreed, Rob disempowered himself by stating that his backer had set limits that he could not pass. He also stated that his backer was only interested in a deal if it was completed by the end of March, which barely offered enough time for any legal work to be completed. He managed to maintain a collaborative relationship by separating himself from the terms set out by his backer without ever exposing his backer. Rob calculated that the value that the restaurant and facilities would bring to the Marina in enhanced facilities and appeal would be considerable, so demanded a 5-year rent-free deal in return for a £500,000 investment in the infrastructure of the building and facilities. He sold 50% of his business for £550,000 to his backer, who continues to this day to serve as Rob's "higher authority." The £50,000 balance was used for operating expenses.

STARTING WITH TOP-TO-TOP AGREEMENTS

Top-to-top meetings serve to set the tone, promote and reinforce trust, as well as setting parameters of pending negotiations. They also provide the opportunity to pre-condition the other party by setting out expectations without getting drawn into finite detail.

Ligo, a sports clothing brand, decided to renegotiate a new set of terms with their 18 main distributors across Europe. The changes that required renegotiation included volumes, discount structures, advertising, information sharing, payment terms, and order lead times.

Ultimately, their distributors would be facing a price increase via an "updated discount structure," which Ligo needed to implement to fund their significant marketing campaign. The benefit to the distributors would be increased volume orders. They knew the negotiations were going to be tough. Eighty percent of their business was with their five largest distributors so the size and importance of these were the primary focus for the leaders of Ligo.

The strategy adopted by Ligo involved top-to-top meetings to discuss new product lines, reliability of delivery lead times, and a uniform transparent discount structure. These messages were sold without mention of specific details. The directors insisted that both parties had teams who could work through "the detail." They focused on the new lines and the need to provide fair, transparent discounting for all their distributors, which would help their customers' businesses grow.

Essentially, they had paved the way for negotiations by disempowering themselves and not becoming drawn on details. Had they not done so, they would have compromised their strategy and potentially faced demands, because their distributors would have known that it was ultimately the directors that set the terms in the first place.

EMPOWERMENT WITHIN TEAM ROLES

When negotiating in teams it is important to be organized in such a way that you perform well as a unit. Understanding who is empowered to do what and who will take the final decisions is also key to the workings of any team in pressured situations. Negotiating in teams can only be effective when everyone understands and keeps to their role, and is able to contribute towards the team's efforts. There are four distinct team roles that are typically adopted:

- the spokesperson;
- the figures person;
- the observer; and
- the leader.

Each is designed to help your team perform to the best of its varied abilities.

The spokesperson

The spokesperson is empowered. Their role is to:

- conduct most of the dialogue;
- table proposals within agreed parameters with the leader in the negotiation team; and
- trade variables on behalf of the team, while still needing to refer to their leader to get final agreement.

That is not to say that others should not or cannot talk, but they should do so through invitation from the spokesperson. The team is there to support the spokesperson.

The figures person

The figures person should not typically be involved in the dialog unless invited to do so. They:

- understand the implications of movement on each of the variables;
- advise on possibilities, calculate movements, possibilities, and proposals;
- understand the total value of the agreement at any given point in time; and
- advise the leader as the negotiation proceeds.

The observer

The observer is also disempowered. Their role is to:

- watch and monitor the other party;
- hear the things that others may be too preoccupied to hear;
- understand the motives, interests, and priorities of the other party; and
- read the size, timing, and nature of the moves that are taking place.

The purpose of the role is to help you to understand what is driving the other party. The observer is your eyes and ears in the room. They generally workout what's happening in the room when others are too preoccupied.

The leader

The leader is usually the person with the greatest level of authority. They are the person who speaks least, but speaks loudest. Their role is to:

- set out the agenda and form the climate for the meeting;
- allow the spokesperson to manage the trading on behalf of the team; and
- summarize from time to time where clarity is required and make the final decision.

However, the leader is not the negotiator. This task is delegated to the spokesperson, who is the voice of the team.

More than four

Often the team is larger than four members. More frequently, you will have to play all four roles yourself, at the same time. This makes your task of negotiating more demanding because there are many things to think about, consider, and respond to. This is one of the reasons why preparation is so important to negotiators. You should never think on your feet, never seek to rush the deal, and always understand the pace at which you can operate and manage your meetings accordingly.

For some, disempowerment feels like a straitjacket – for others, a suit of armor. It works both ways and is used by companies to expand or narrow the scope and risk. It is used as a tactic to protect or deflect conflict, as well as a negotiating lever.

Even a pilot landing their aircraft will take instructions from air traffic control regarding flight path, timings, and other relevant instructions during descent. They are part of a team and different members of the team will carry different forms of responsibility and will be empowered to make certain decisions. Fortunately, everything the pilot does can be seen by everyone who has an interest in their activity.

GETTING EMPOWERED BEFORE YOU START

Often before negotiations start, you may find yourself involved in internal negotiations to agree your parameters and how far you are authorized to go, or whether you will entertain discussions on particular variables as part of concluding an agreement. This is an important part of the planning process. Without these parameters, you could in theory become dangerous because you could agree to anything. So, degrees of empowerment are usually put in place to protect you (providing you with a basis for trading), and to protect your businesses.

Equally, the other party will have parameters within which they can operate. It is quite common for some people to open a negotiation discussion outlining the areas that are non-negotiable "deal breakers" and the areas that are available for discussion. The likelihood is that they are either not empowered to negotiate over certain areas because of the parameters that have been set, or they have decided for now to introduce such parameters, allowing them to broaden the agenda during later discussions.

DEFENSE IN DEPTH

The seller says: "If you can agree to a price of $19 a unit on 30 days delivery, we will agree to payment terms of 30 days." The buyer says "I am able to agree to that, but I just need to run that past my boss as it is above my authorization level, I'll call you this afternoon." That afternoon, the buyer calls the salesman: "Good news, my boss says that if you can agree to $18 a unit he will sign it off." The salesman sees this as a tactic they have come across before, called "defense in depth." However, he needs the deal, so yields to the offer: "OK, but I need a confirmation in writing back by the morning." "That's great," says the buyer, "We can now put the agreement before the head of buying for the final sign-off and I'll have it back to you by the morning." The following morning arrives and the buyer calls the seller. "The head of buying says that if the deal meets our standard payment terms of 45 days, he will sign the agreement. Of course I would have signed it off, but it's out of my hands now." The seller is so close and because he is empowered to authorize the 45 days, he agrees, "Just sign it and get it back to me."

The pressure the salesman is under to get the agreement signed, and the fact that he works for an "empowering" sales organization, has resulted in the salesman's position being compromised. Had he been disempowered to move beyond certain predefined limits, the buyer may well have had to review his approach or renegotiated on other variables. This higher authority tactic is used frequently where one party does not qualify the decision-making process beyond the person they are dealing with, leaving themselves exposed to further negotiations.

DECISION-MAKING AUTHORITY
Linking empowerment to accountability

ENSURING THE NEGOTIATOR IS ACCOUNTABLE FOR THE "TOTAL VALUE"

A manufacturer was involved in a negotiation to supply safety helmets for a new construction site. Their contact was a procurement

(Continued)

manager who needed to place an order for two sizes of helmet, which had to meet specific health and safety standards.

- The safety helmets were to be used at a new construction site due to accommodate over 700 contractors.
- The helmets needed to be delivered on site within 4 weeks, when the contractors were due to arrive and the next health and safety inspection was due.
- The owners of the site managed a number of other sites, some of which were due to be started in the next few months.

The procurement manager had narrowed down the potential suppliers to two known manufacturers and then commenced his negotiations. The first supplier offered a very keen price, subject to preferred supplier status and a guaranteed order to supply the remaining four other sites to be launched, at the same price per unit. The second supplier did not ask for the longer-term order, was 5% more expensive, and could not deliver for 5 weeks.

The procurement manager's instincts were to go with the first offer. However, he then considered what risks this might entail. The first supplier was cheaper but what were the implications if they were to deliver late? The costs could be hundreds of times the price of the order. He double-checked the specification, trying to work out why they were so cheap. What would the implications be if the hats did not meet the required specifications? The risks of failing to meet the health and safety requirements meant this deal was not just about the hats. It was about the total site being ready to operate, which meant having them ready and available to wear. The procurement manager referred to his boss to discuss the merits of the options. Ultimately they requested written guarantees from both suppliers and recognition of the consequences of late delivery. Not surprisingly, only the second supplier responded and so secured the order.

Any individual who is empowered to negotiate the best deal must also be made accountable for the broader implications of their agreements; otherwise what looks like a great deal could turn out to be a disaster for the organization. The challenge for the empowered negotiator is therefore to understand and negotiate/mitigate for the risks and, when in doubt, escalate.

EMPOWERMENT AND SCOPE TO CREATE VALUE

So, responsibility and accountability go hand in hand. Some businesses want their managers to be entrepreneurial. They want to empower them to take decisions, to be creative, to build agreements, and to maximize value within the agreements they are involved in.

In fact, high-potential deals come from creative thinking (trait 9, Chapter 4). Creative thinking comes from those who are empowered and therefore encouraged to think more broadly. If you disempower someone by providing them with limited scope to operate, it will limit their thinking and attract responses such as: "I didn't even consider the prospect of a joint venture; it's not part of my remit."

If you want to negotiate incremental value in your agreements you need to be empowered with as much scope as possible.

The importance of defining value

Having greater scope with moderate forms of empowerment offers a balance which many organizations adopt. However, scope and creativity must also be linked to accountability. You might ask someone to build creative deals that maximize value. However, unless you define *how* value will be measured, they may overlook the risks they have accepted in their quest to extract value. If the personal benefits associated with highly profitable agreements are very high, limits of authority may be worth building into the negotiator's brief. As we have witnessed in the global banking industry in the lead-up to the credit crunch during 2008/9, individuals will entertain risk in the quest for personal gain, especially when they are authorized to do so.

KEY TAKEAWAYS

Empowerment works just like authority. The more empowered you are, the more scope you have to negotiate. The positives are that with greater scope you can be more creative by working with a broader agenda and more variables. The negatives are that you can become exposed to pressure because you are empowered to say yes. In other words it is often those with the authority who need protecting, which is why the act of negotiation is often delegated to others.

- Seek a higher authority as a way of disempowering yourself when necessary.
- Agree to whom and when you should escalate discussions or decision making before you start.
- Agree (and negotiate if necessary) the scope and parameters of your empowerment before you start.
- Always qualify the level of empowerment of those you are dealing with.
- When they say *they* are unable to agree, seek to escalate the matter to someone who can.
- Agreed team roles and discipline provides greater protection from tactics others may use.
- If you are empowered to negotiate around a broad range of variables, understand the value of each issue from inside the other party's head.

CHAPTER 8

Tactics and Values

"Experience is not what happens to you; it's what you do with what happens to you."

Aldous Huxley

The decisions you take and the way you behave during your negotiations will be influenced by how much power you think you have and by the way your own values or ethics influence your behavior.

The tactics you employ will be limited by both how much power you have, whether you have a short- or long-term relationship to consider and this may influence how ethical you choose to be during your negotiations.

The dilemma of where the value of fairness fits into negotiation has challenged many organizations. For instance, some organizations who hold strong views on being fair and reasonable may take exception when faced with a trading partner who behaves in a manipulative or irrational manner. On principle, they will not tolerate the behavior and will exit the relationship.

RECOGNIZING THE PROCESS AND THE GAMESMANSHIP IN PLAY

The way the balance of power is split, and how it shifts with time and circumstance, means you cannot expect agreements always to be, or appear to be, balanced and fair, or even consistent. You can, however, work towards getting the best possible deal given the circumstances you face. Some, faced with such situations, turn to tactics and some become victims of the tactics in play. The Complete Skilled Negotiator sees them for what they are and where necessary uses counter tactics to neutralize their effects.

I am not implying here what is right or wrong. You will conduct business based on values that are probably different from those of others. This does not make yours right or wrong; it does not make the other party's values right or wrong. It simply means that our interpretation, understanding, and use of tactics will differ from others as the implications of making use of them will differ based on your circumstances and our view of what acceptable behavior is made up of.

As a general rule, negotiations that focus on short-term agreements with parties with whom we have no ongoing relationship, or prospect of one in the future, are more inclined to gravitate towards value distribution (1–6 o'clock) negotiations. Tactics tend to be more readily used in these styles of negotiations as the relationships involved tend not to be long term.

A QUESTION OF CHOICES AND PERSONAL STYLE

The concept of "fairness" is exploited by some negotiators through the use of tactics. Western democratic societies are designed to offer freedom and choice. This serves to remove the notion of being controlled, and, as long as we have choices, many perceive this as freedom and fairness. So choices are designed to signal fairness. However, if like governments you are *controlling* the options or choices, then you have the power to influence the outcome.

However, if you are overtly unfair in the choices you provide others, trust will be difficult to build and, with no trust, it is difficult to negotiate collaboratively (7–12 o'clock on the clock face).

Social laws, or the unwritten laws of society, influence our view of what is fair and reasonable under whatever circumstances. Business partnerships, where there is a need to maintain productive relationships and the need to jointly problem solve or develop incremental value by working together, require at least some level of trust.

To be perceived to be fair in business, you need to offer choices: choices that are not so one-sided that they quickly become regarded transparent and unfair.

Personal attributes

Your personal values and how they influence your behavior will have a powerful bearing on where you and the other party gravitate to on the clock face. They can, if not managed, directly influence whether you build relationships or whether you enter into combat each time you seek to agree terms. Below are some of the personal attributes to consider and the influence they will exert during your negotiations.

Trust in business has to be earned and is easily broken. It implies that you are good for your word. If you say something will happen, it happens, consistently. You approach the conversation from their perspective, sharing their concerns and working on the problems that you both identify, together. It does not mean that you have to pay by conceding on terms, by offering personal favors or by being more transparent with your interests.

Respect comes from being firm, consistent and reliable. If you are too flexible or concede too easily, the other party will regard you as being weak. In negotiation, everything is possible, but difficult. The fact that it is difficult ensures that the work you put into the deal, engineering the terms, and moving reluctantly, attracts respect for you, your position and your credibility.

Integrity comes from consistency. This can present issues for negotiators who are too focused on not being unpredictable. Maintaining confidentiality and being reliable, in that you follow through with your commitments, also help promote integrity, which in some relationships or even industries is critical if business is to take place at all.

Honesty. You never need to lie in negotiation. You don't need to tell them what you won't do. Focus on what you will do. Think "how" or "on what basis could we, or could they?" By telling them what you are prepared to do you are at least maintaining honesty. By telling them you are prepared to pay $100 when you know that you could pay $150 is not lying. Don't confuse the process of negotiation with lying and telling the truth. If you lie in negotiation, you could be taking unnecessary risks, and in some cases completely compromising relationships, however, don't expect everyone to adhere to this discipline.

Consideration of the needs of the other party. If you don't understand these you are not ready to negotiate. Your planning, preparation, research, and exploration meetings are all there to help you to establish their position, motives, priorities, and interests. To place a value on these you have to understand the deal the way they do business from inside their head. Considering the facts will allow you to remain sensitive to the issues and respectful where necessary.

Empathy is about understanding and appreciating the challenges from their perspective, but never compromising because of such understandings.

Responsibility. It is you who will conduct your negotiations and you who will make the decisions with the authority limits you have been given. The more trust that genuinely exists within your relationships, the more scope you have to open up the agenda and work together creatively. This will only come about if you cultivate the necessary climate and discussions.

Risky attributes

Openness. This can be dangerous in negotiation. Information is power and the more you share with the other party, the more you will expose yourself. Be open but stay within the parameters that you set yourself. If you don't understand this from the outset you will place yourself in a very vulnerable position.

Compassion. In the tough world of business your job is to maximize opportunity. You will do this with those you can work with and rely on, and who remain highly competitive. This is a capitalist market we operate in. Compassion, like generosity, has to take a back seat once a negotiation commences unless of course you have a longer-term plan in mind.

WHAT ARE TACTICS?

When do tactics usually come into play?

Tactics tend to be used more frequently when one party has more power than the other and tries to take advantage of it. Tactics are also more frequently used where the nature of the negotiation is based on value distribution and the focus is on taking as much value off the table as possible.

Dealing with tactics and when to use them

There are dozens of books written on negotiation that present tactics as the basis of negotiation. They are given names that serve to explain the approach: "The Russian front," "The Trojan horse," and so on. The most important thing about tactics is to recognize them for what they are.

- They are neither clever nor sophisticated.
- They are designed to apply pressure and usually by those who can because they have enough power, or think they have enough power, to do so, or those who think they are clever enough to do so without any consequences.

However, they are used with such regularity that one has to recognize and understand them, adapt to them, and, where necessary and appropriate, even use them. To help with this I have categorized a range of tactics using a simple scale of 1–10 (1 is low and 10 is high) against two factors:

- **Power required**: the amount of power you will need to have or be perceived to have relative to the other party for this tactic to work.
- **Relationship erosion**: the degree to which your relationship or any trust that may exist within it will be eroded, if the tactic once used becomes obvious or transparent to the other party.

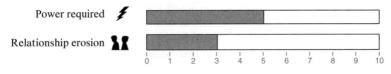

Figure 8.1 Tactics scale.

For the purpose of outlining some of the more widely used tactics, I have placed them into one of seven categories. These are:

	Tactics
1. Information	- "The hypothetical question" - "Off the record" - Full disclosure and openness - Why?
2. Time and momentum	- Deadlines - "And just one more thing" - Denied access - Time constraint - The auction - Time out
3. Fear or guilt	- Physically disturbing them - Good guy, bad guy - The Russian front - Personal favor - Guilty party - The social smell - Silence
4. Anchoring	- Sow the seed early - The power statement - The mock shock - The professional flinch - The broken record
5. Empowerment	- Higher authority - Defense in depth - Use of official authority - "It's all I can afford" - Onus transfer - Off-limits - New faces

	Tactics
6. Moving the costs around	- The building block technique - Wipe the proposal off the table without saying no - Linking the issues - Side issue or red herring - The slice
7. Deceit	- Trojan horse - The incorrect summary - Deliberate misunderstanding - The dumb foreigner - The loss leader

1. Information

Information is power. The more information you have about the options, circumstances, and priorities of the other party, the more powerful you become.

"The hypothetical question"

"What if . . . " and "Suppose that . . . " questions used during the exploratory and closing stages can help you to work out the degree of flexibility the other party is prepared to offer, or the relative value of the issues being discussed.

For example: "What if we were to 'hypothetically' increase the order after 3 months, how might that change the fee structure?" There may be no intention of doing so, but the idea is to test assumptions, gain insights and untimately trade more effectively later on during your negotiation. It can be used to explore possibilities, especially where deadlock is looming.

"Off the record"

This is where one party asks the other for a view, a comment, or to simply share an insight, in the name of helping both parties make progress. Their intentions may be genuine, but the information is sought for one reason only: to get inside your head. You may choose to use it yourself for the same reason. However, when asked for an "off the record" meeting, always remember the real risks you carry. Any indications, signals, comments, or even attitudes you imply will be read into. There is no such thing as an "off the record" meeting. Anything you tell them or their business will quickly make its way to the decision maker and is likely to influence the outcome. By all means make use of "off the record," but do not get used by it.

Full disclosure and openness

When a request for full disclosure is made before or during a meeting, there needs to be a reasonable degree of trust or mutual dependency before parties tend to agree. Even then it usually comes with conditions or limits: "We will share our data with you on the current site, but feel that extending this to our overall operation to be unnecessary," is the type of response you will get. Some will say: "I'm going to be really open with you," which usually means they are not. This is also the case when people use such words as "really," "actually," "genuinely," "seriously," "sincerely," and, most common of all, "honestly." Whenever I have heard these words in negotiation where people are under pressure, I have concluded that the truth has not been in play. Listen out for them and remain mindful of the longer-term implications of full disclosure.

In reality, you can assume that something will usually be held back. The process of due diligence is used for very good reasons: to ensure the integrity of information provided is true and complete.

Why?

This simple question can be used to challenge everything from interests, priorities, agenda items or even new proposals. It has been used as an effective way of establishing the thinking and importance of any issue or statement. Anyone can ask "why?", which is why curious children ask it time after time in their quest for knowledge. The information you receive will always provide an insight, even if it's something like: "We are not prepared to go into detail on that issue." During exploration discussions, it's worth asking why the other party is asking the very question that they are; and what insight this gives you into their thinking.

2. Time and momentum

Time is the most powerful lever available to any negotiator. Time and circumstances affect the value of just about every product or service bought and sold around the world. If I was going to provide you with a full advertising plan to support your June election campaign, but could not actually start until June, my services would be deemed useless and without value. However, if the service could commence in during March, and run for 3 months peaking with tailored activity throughout June, the service could attract a premium. It's the same service with a different time slot, which makes all the difference. So, understanding the time pressures of the other party is vital to you being able to optimize the leverage during your negotiations. How you communicate your own time pressures or use the other party's time pressures to gain movement or agreement can be directly influenced by the tactics you use.

Deadlines

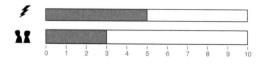

"If you do not agree by Friday we will not be able to start the project in the timescales you have stipulated."

"We are closing the book on this one so we will need to know by this afternoon if you want to take part."

"If we can agree in principle today, I will ensure you get the business, subject to us 'ironing out' the terms."

The pressure that deadlines can exert means that some may not only use this tactic as a closing device, but also to provide you with the feeling of having "won." Deadlines are used in many other ways, for example: "Because of changes in our business, after today's deadline, any agreement will have to be signed off by my boss." On some occasions, once the other party has established your deadlines they will employ this need as a trading variable. They will imply that the timing issue is not so critical to them. Be careful when providing total transparency relating to the implications of deadlines; it can be a highly effective and manipulative tool.

"And just one more thing"

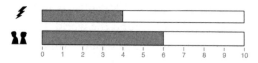

This is often used at the end of the negotiation when the deal is regarded as all but done. One party turns to the other just as you are about to shake hands and says: "Just one more thing, you will of course be including the flexible payment scheduling we discussed earlier?" They pause and wait with their hand held out. You think, I'm there, deal done, finished, closed. Do I now open up the discussion again, or worse still, compromise the agreement by saying "no, but I didn't think that flexible payment scheduling was ever part of the terms we had agreed."

As you can see, this tactic has a higher relationship erosion factor. If the other party has either power or enough nerve, they will and should challenge the assumption by attaching a condition to the flexible payment scheduling in the same way they would have if it had been raised earlier during the formal discussions.

Denied access

When you need to move discussions on, perhaps due to time pressure or the implications of deadlines, some will use denied access as a tactic. They simply ensure they are not available. They tell their colleagues and assistants to pass on the message they are in back-to-back meetings, out of town, away, or anything that ensures that you, the other party, cannot make progress until they are ready.

One way of dealing with this situation when you are confident that denied access is in play is to leave a message for the other party, bringing your deadline artificially forward, adding that if the deadline passes without agreement, the deal is off or the terms on offer are time limited. Although risky, this buys you a window of opportunity between the deadline they think you are working to and the one actually in play. Another is to introduce a credible option, perhaps another party or option that you plan to take up and you need to let them know within certain timescales. If you don't hear back you will place the order, reluctantly, elsewhere. Of course these options carry risks but often work as a way of unlocking the denied access tactic.

Time constraint

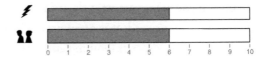

This is used where the other party introduces artificial time lines or deadlines, stating that their offer expires on a certain date. Further demands are then introduced as a consequence of the deadline not being met as "compensation" against the implications.

Time constraints are also used where one party is near agreement on most of the terms, but the other decides to hold out for a better fee rate. They say: "We will give you one last chance to increase your offer. Please advise us by 5.30 pm on Friday of what this is, and we'll let you know if we are prepared to progress." During the time that passes, which is aimed at fuelling uncertainty and doubt, the other party is often pressured into improving their final offer.

The auction

The bidding process is designed to create competition. The process is engineered and controlled by the organizers. As the bids increase, rational judgment is tested and for those with high egos, winning has been known to take over as the predominant driver of behavior. Time and momentum work against those willing to continue bidding, so a clear and absolute break point must feature as part of your planning if you are to enter such a process.

Time out

When in doubt, for whatever reason, adjourn the meeting and take a time out to regroup. You need to understand the implications, risks, or finances if you are to maintain clarity and be able to work out how you are going to move forward. It is often used when new information comes to the fore, or if deadlock is looming and a need for a "fresh look" at the deal is needed. It's also used when time is running out and one party chooses to put the other under pressure by removing themselves from the room until time pressures become critical.

3. Fear or guilt

This next category raises the stakes in the relationship and heightens the risk. With high levels of power, threats are used in subtle ways to create movement. It is the fear of these threats or the fear of losing the deal that is played upon by those seeking to manipulate the power they have.

Physically disturbing them

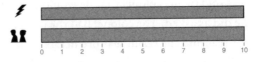

This is made up of a variety of non-violent but yet physical gestures which are introduced to unsettle and distract you. This can include leaning across the table to invade your personal space, sitting very close to you, or changing the seating pattern, so they are sat next to you. Seating positioned to face the sunlight or groups crammed into very small rooms are all part of the environment used to intimidate. Always remember that you are in charge and that includes your environment, so if it does not feel right, challenge it, question it and change it. You'll attract respect for doing so and set the scene for equal respect in the meeting.

Good guy, bad guy

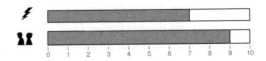

This is typically used in team negotiations where one member of the team makes very high or irrational demands, and the other offers a more reasonable approach; or one is challenging and dismissive whilst their colleague presents themselves as far more understanding. The approach is designed to make the "good guys" appear reasonable, rational, and understanding, and therefore all the more agreeable. Essentially it's using the law of relativity to attract cooperation. It's transparent enough and certainly erodes any potential for trust, so ensure next time you are exposed to it that you see it for what it is.

The Russian front

As described by Gavin Kennedy in his book *Everything is Negotiable*, this tactic is taken from the Second World War where a Russian lieutenant was told by his colonel that he would be sent to the Russian front unless he did as asked. The colonel had the power, the lieutenant believed it was for real, and the result was predictable. He would do whatever was asked willingly, rather than being sent to the Russian front. In negotiation, it is referred to when providing two options. This is based on getting the other party to accept the better of two evils. One you know will prove challenging and the other an outright disaster. If the whole concept is not rejected, the chances are you will be seduced into agreeing to the challenging one.

Personal favor

This tactic attempts to make the position or request "personal" and works most effectively in familiar relationships: "You can do this for old times' sake," or "If you do this for me I will ensure your proposal is accepted," or "You scratch my back and I'll scratch yours." It leans on a sense of obligation to the point where it's aimed at leaving you feeling embarrassed if you do not yield. You must remain firm, point out the compromising position this would leave you in and explain that it's not personal, just business.

Guilty party

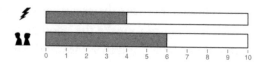

This involves suggesting that the other party is breaking some code or agreement, or that they are going against the industry norm, or that a commitment has not been met or a performance not as it should be. This tactic is used to full effect where one party is negotiating compensation to include inconvenience, loss of face, indirect loss of earnings, even future risk; this results in a demand way beyond the normal financial obligations.

The social smell

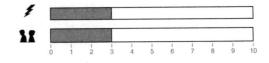

The social smell is used to imply that you are the odd one out. It's designed to make you question your own judgment: "If everyone else is behaving in a certain way (agreeing), why am I not?" It comes in the form of a statement about what "others are doing" and importantly what you are not. It implies that you are out of sync, the odd one out, and that you are missing out or even being irrational. "Everyone else has committed ... you'll be the only one not included so you are likely to miss out whilst your competitors have all agreed." The idea is that it helps apply pressure to conform, highlights isolation, and promotes self-doubt.

Silence

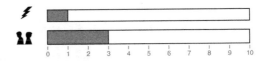

As a powerful tactic, silence is used to unnerve the other party. It can result in a waiting game because the first to talk is likely to be the first to concede. For many, the discomfort alone of continued silence can result in a concession or offer of further flexibility. And yet for the experienced negotiator it may be that they simply need time to think through their next move. Silence is best used directly after you have stated your proposal or after they have stated theirs. Just wait. Even if they respond, wait further. The pressure builds and often leads to more concessions.

4. Anchoring

This is where one party sets out to form an anchor (an opening position taken up by one party from which they will move but such movement will come at a price). The aim of anchoring is to adjust the expectations of the other party providing an extreme and yet realistic opening position. Movement becomes relative to the anchor. If you open with your position first and are able to get the other party talking about it, even if this means them rejecting it, it is your position that becomes anchored in their mind. Unless they make a counter-offer. Often they become so preoccupied with attacking your position, they forget all about their own position.

Sow the seed early

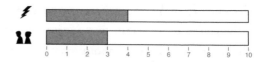

This can take the form of the advance telephone call, which is designed to introduce an idea or a position, allowing for any emotional reaction to take place prior to the meeting. Or ideas that are introduced and parked in earlier meetings in the knowledge that they will need to be addressed in subsequent meetings. Sowing the seed early is based on getting inside their heads and adjusting their expectations.

The power statement

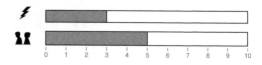

Opening statements are designed to manage the aspirations of the other party. They are usually used as a statement in the form of an assumed fact. The idea is to test an assumed position of power by effectively telling them that, whilst you are in a position of "indifference," they are under pressure to conclude the deal with you: "I understand that you need an agreement in place by the end of the day," or "I want to make it clear that today's discussions are to ensure that we have given you every opportunity to win the business." The language is that used by a "critical parent" by implying assumed authority designed to get the other party talking and thinking about how they are going to move towards you.

The mock shock

This is an extension to the power statement where you start the meeting by implying that all is lost: "We have decided that given your current performance levels and clearly no desire to offer compensation, terminating the contract is the only option for us." Or, "This may only be a small order, but failure to agree could affect all of your business with us." The devastating consequences of non-cooperation can shock the other party into reconsidering their position or backtracking from the outset, where saving the relationship becomes their primary objective.

The professional flinch

This is a shock reaction to their opening position. Both physically whether by extreme facial reaction and/or verbally, you are demonstrating your shock and surprise at their position. Used regardless of their opening offer and designed to lower their aspirations, the professional flinch has the effect of undermining their confidence in their position and expectations.

The broken record

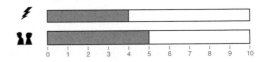

One party repeats their position. The more they repeat it, the more credible it becomes. The more their position is discussed, the more likely the discussion will revolve around their position. They start to sound like a broken record but the message gets through. Of course this can be interpreted as intransigence and can result in you losing patience and concluding the meeting. They will require a moderate amount of power of around 4/10 to be able to carry it off.

5. Empowerment

This involves the degree to which you are authorized to trade (see also Chapter 7), and the extent to which others need to be involved in the decision-making process.

Higher authority

The use of the boss or a mysterious and distant overseeing body required to sign off anything beyond those limits that you are allowed to trade. The idea is to convince the other party to agree within the level you are authorized to go to, so that they can complete the deal today, rather than risk the deal being jeopardized, or so as not to allow your boss to see the other concessions that you have already offered. It's also used to disassociate yourself from not being able to accept a proposal: "That's out of my control and I will need to come back to you on that one."

Defense in depth

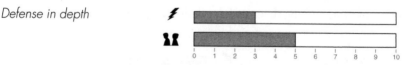

This is where several layers of decision-making authority allow for further conditions to be applied each time the agreement is referred. Typically it's where your supplier or customer states that they will take the deal for sign-off to their boss. A day later, the call comes that, subject to one final concession, the deal will be agreed. You reluctantly agree. A day later, they call and state that their boss has signed it off and it's now been sent for approval to the board and that if you could just agree to the 30-day payment terms it will gain agreement. Reluctantly you agree and ask if they will let you know when it has been approved. The next day they calls to again advise you that the board have now signed it off and they have now handed it over to Health and Safety for final approval and then advise you of yet another small concession that will be necessary if "final" sign-off is to be achieved. You should always understand the decision-making levels and process, otherwise you leave yourself exposed to defense in depth.

Use of official authority

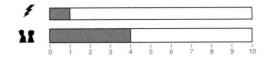

This is used where one party disempowers themselves, saying that they cannot or are not allowed to change the terms. They refer to their own company policy, legal requirements, association requirements, or even historical precedents and, although sometimes true, it's often a tactic in play used to legitimize their position. "Our company policy is 60 days payment on all transactions and there is nothing we can do about that." It's frequently used to provide rationale in an attempt to bolster the credibility of their proposal. Ensure you insist that such constraints are their problem and that you welcome suggestions on how they plan to work around them in order to avoid you having to escalate the issue.

"It's all I can afford"

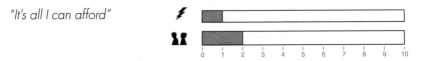

This is used to suggest that budgets are finite, the specification is fixed, and that it's all that is available: "I have no other funds available so take it or leave it." It's designed to place the onus of obligation on the other party, implying that they need to work within that which you can afford. In contrast, when faced with such tactics the receiving party can change the specification, the volume, the timing, or any variable that helps to naturalize the implications of the fixed fee.

Onus transfer

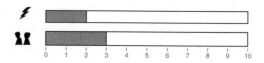

Transferring the obligation for solutions or ideas onto the other party, to make it their problem. "We have a problem in making our payment on time this month. We can make the transfer but it is going to be 5 days late, how do you want to deal with this?" Once they have been advised, the problem becomes a shared one. The implications may still sit squarely with you but you have transferred the onus onto the other party.

Off-limits

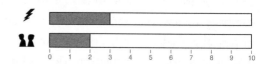

This is where issues are positioned as off-limits (non-negotiable or "off the agenda" for the purpose of these discussions). They are often described as "things I can't agree, so let's focus on the terms we can agree today." Remember, nothing is agreed until everything is agreed. Their motive is to protect some of the more critical issues from negotiation. This can also result in a negotiation over what is negotiable before the real negotiation even begins. This tactic is commonly used in political negotiations but regularly features in all types of commercial settlement negotiations too.

New faces

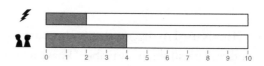

When a new person takes over the relationship or a new account manager is introduced, both past precedents and history carry far less relevance. New faces need not be tied to or constrained by what has happened in the past. They can sometimes offer a solution to deadlock where personalities stand in the way of progress. They can provide for a fresh examination of affairs or can even be used to intimidate the other party where the seniority of the new negotiator carries certain gravitas. Retailers are renowned for changing their buyers systematically and periodically so that new faces remove the familiarity of an existing trading relationship. This keeps the focus on terms fresh and removes any scope for complacency.

6. Moving the costs around

This category comes from reconfiguring the package or specification, or manipulating the terms in order to provide a different complexion to the deal. The relationship between specification and price is used by many tactical negotiators as a means of manipulating the cost of supply, whilst attracting the best possible price.

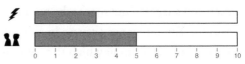

The building block technique

This is where one party requests a price but only for part of their actual requirements. You then request prices for various quantity arrangements, ranging up to and including your actual needs. The idea is to manage expectations in the first instance and understand the relative cost/price differences and implications across the different arrangements. This can reveal much about their cost base and margin structure. You then negotiate for a 1-year agreement, for example, in the knowledge that you can raise this to a 3-year agreement. You then seek incentives from the other party in the event that you could extend the agreement to 2 years, and then negotiate incremental terms for this "doubling" of the contract.

Finally, you broaden the discussion to a 3-year partnership. Of course, to agree to such a deal, you will require more preferential terms.

The building block technique involves planning out your stages, which can apply to any variable and provides time for the other party to adjust to concessions that would otherwise be difficult to extract.

Wipe their proposal off the
table without saying no

Each time they make a proposal, you say "yes, subject to our terms."

Your terms turn out to be either equally as outrageous, or are financially designed to offset the implications of agreeing to them. One party says: "Your discount levels based on last year's performance are being adjusted from 10% to 7.5% for the year ahead." And the other party responds: "Subject to you improving your promotional funding from $100,000 to $250,000 for the year, we will accept the reduction in discount."

The response from the first party will inevitably be: "We can't do that" to which you suggest: "and that's why we are not in a position to accept your position." You rarely need say no in a negotiation. Just find a way, a basis, a set of conditions upon which the consequences, be they financial, risk, or third-party implications, are neutralized by the terms you attach to it.

Linking the issues

Everything is conditional and therefore linked to other conditions. Linking the relative values and importance of issues is key to ensuring that linked issues gain the attention you require. This is sometimes used to protect certain terms. For example, if the contract length was very important to one party and they knew that a high-value variable to the other party was attracting a 10,000-volume order, the two would be linked to ensure that the contract length issues could not be easily dismissed.

Side issue or red herring

This is where some issues are introduced onto the agenda that have been positioned to lose or trade off against. Later during the negotiation, value is traded as each of the red herrings is conceded, having played their part in attracting improved terms elsewhere. For example, you need to attract shorter lead times and improved discounts. Both items are on the agenda as is a new termination clause, allowing you to terminate the contract with very short notice and lower volume discount thresholds. The last two are effectively red herrings, which you expect to concede on. However, in doing so you are able to trade for better terms on lead times and discounts.

The slice

This is where you believe that the issue is of high value to the other party and trade against the issue in "slices." For example, you know that volume is critical to them. You are currently at 50,000 units and know that your requirement is for an order of 150,000 units. Rather than trade up to 150,000 units, you trade to 80,000 in return for a concession. Later you trade to 100,000 for a further concession, then to 115,000, and so on. Each move is conditional on a concession, ensuring that the value of your total move is maximized.

7. Deceit

There is no other way to describe this final category: deceit. If reputation or relationships hold any value to you or your business, think twice before using the following. More importantly, be wary of those who carry a different view and choose to use deceit – they may choose to use it on you even after the contract has been signed.

Trojan horse

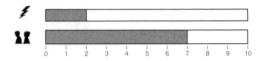

This is named after a tactic used during the ancient war on Troy, which led to the saying: "Beware of Greeks bearing gifts." The Greeks left a gift in the form of a wooden horse outside Troy. The Trojans accepted the gift and brought it inside the city only to find that the horse was full of soldiers ready to invade. Beware if the deal appears too good to be true. This relates to the hidden small print, and the conditions and issues that can literally come out of the woodwork after the deal has been completed. The Trojan horse represents a package created to entice you. Once accepted, it has some surprises in store because much of the downside was hidden at the time of agreement.

The incorrect summary

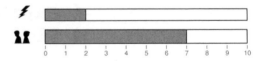

This is where one party summarizes from their perspective, leaving out or even adjusting some of the terms discussed earlier. The idea is that you won't notice or won't challenge through fear of jeopardizing progress. Try to ensure that you summarize progress throughout the meeting and that you do so from your perspective. Also, ensure that you summarize in writing after the meeting. If you don't agree on what you believe you have agreed, then you're unlikely to have an agreement that is going to stand the test of time.

Deliberate misunderstanding

So as to open up areas that have already been regarded as concluded, one party introduces a condition that they know to be unacceptable. After you have responded with confusion or start to demand clarity they adopt an "innocent misunderstanding" stance. Their motives could be varied, but it is usually related to stalling progress or allowing them to try and renegotiate terms that have otherwise been regarded as closed.

The dumb foreigner

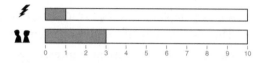

They choose not to understand you at a given time during the negotiation due to language difficulty. This is especially used once the subject of price is introduced. As they seek to take up a firm position, they appear increasingly confused by what you have to say as you attempt to explain your position. When faced with such behavior, patience, restating your position, and maybe even a "time out" is needed to dampen their confidence.

The loss leader

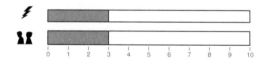

This involves one party convincing the other to agree to a deal at highly preferential rates, which will lead to benefits in the future. These "benefits" are often not contractual, conditional, or delivered on. In fact they are often used as a precedent: "You were able to offer that price last time we worked with you so we know you can do it again." If you are to enter into such agreements always ensure that it is in writing and the conditions are clearly stated in the contract.

KEY TAKEAWAYS
Influential tactics in negotiation have been used for thousands of years as a means of gaining leverage and advantage. They can be as subtle as

providing misleading information or as blatant as an outright lie. As you never need to lie in negotiation, many tactics are regarded as a fast route to destroying trust.

- Recognize tactics being used and qualify them by challenging their consequences.
- The type of the tactics you use should be limited to how much trust and dependency you require in the relationship once the deal is done.
- The risk/benefit of employing tactics is something *you must judge* based on your own circumstances, objectives, motivation, and values.
- More than one tactic at a time will often be combined to increase pressure as others will seek to manipulate your actions.
- Performing as a conscious competent negotiator will help increase your awareness of the tactics in play and will help you recognize, qualify, challenge, and navigate through the gamesmanship.

CHAPTER 9

Planning and Preparation that Helps You to Build Value

"There is only one good, knowledge and one evil, ignorance."

Socrates

Planning and preparation is the most fundamental element of negotiating and it is only when the deal is done that the value of this can be fully appreciated. In all my experience I have concluded that there is a direct correlation between how well you have planned the outcome of your negotiations.

To start with it is important not to get confused between knowledge and *ability*. What you understand will help you to perform but this knowledge counts for nothing if you don't possess the motivation to *do*, and that requires making time to plan and prepare. Ignore or avoid this reality at your peril. There will be many reasons, excuses, and time distractions that may impact on your performance as a negotiator. However, if you are disciplined enough to plan and prepare, you will create value and achieve results that would otherwise be beyond your reach.

PLANNING CREATIVE TRADE-OFFS WHICH REALIZE ADDITIONAL VALUE

If you have ever played the game *Tetris* you will know there is a skill involved in getting the right shapes in the right places and in the right order to maximize your score. If you do not adjust the pieces or move the shapes as they become visible they will simply stack up on each other, leaving you with lots of gaps and a low score.

Similarly, in negotiation and working with variables, there is a skill in agreeing to the way and order in which you position the variables. Your motivation, mindset, and flexibility in moving variables around, driven by your planning, provide endless possibilities to maximize value. In the negotiation, the value you create can come from packaging variables together to help realize, protect, or grow the total value available.

As a Complete Skilled Negotiator your planning and preparation will be influenced by the number of variables and possibilities you make use of. This proactive and open-minded approach can provide you with a fundamental advantage in working out what variables might be worth and what each aspect of the deal means to the other party. You would not try to build a house without having completed the drawings, worked through your calculations, and estimated your costs. You would know instinctively that the project would most likely fail without a plan. Negotiation is no different because, once you have started, you should seek to maintain a proactive position and remain in control. Without a plan, you are more likely to be in a reactive position, exposing yourself to circumstances and a position that can easily spiral out of your control.

EACH AND EVERY DEAL IS UNIQUE

Every negotiation you enter will have a set of circumstances surrounding it that effectively make it unique, even those that exist in familiar relationships. Your relationship, timings, market changes, the options you may have, how important the agreement is, and the issues to be agreed will all contribute to the dynamics that create a unique set of circumstances. Working out exactly what it is that is unique to each negotiation you face will also enable you to be creative in your planning. Recognizing this also helps you to get "inside the other person's head," work with a more complex mix of variables with clear financial values, and tackle the more ambiguous or intangible variables, which can often hold the key to additional value.

Even when you have invested in time preparing it's important to realize that, once discussions get under way, you should expect the unexpected. New ideas, consequences, and issues will surface during meetings. These may come in the form of a proposal or a demand you may not have considered before. You will then need to make time to think through the possible implications and, of course, your response. However, because an idea is new, don't reject it because you have yet to consider the implications or cannot calculate the risks immediately. Often there's a signal within the proposal that relates to what's important to the other party. New ideas can also help you to work out what is going on in the other party's head.

UNDERSTANDING VALUE

There are five things that can happen to value in negotiation. You can:

1. give it;
2. create it;
3. share it;
4. protect it; and
5. take it.

As part of your tactical planning you will have considered the clock face and decided on your strategy. If you are planning to increase prices and there are no trade-offs involved, they may regard the negotiation as you simply looking to "take" value. However, before you can impose such a price increase you need to consider the balance of power. For example, the fact that you can tell your kids what to do doesn't mean that it will always be the best thing to do, as you consider the longer-term implications for your relationship. In other words, the more powerful you are, the more options you have, but you need to remain mindful of the longer-term dependency in play.

The three dynamics of value

In negotiation, as in business, the general offer is that you can have "it" quick, good, or cheap. Now pick any two.

In other words, if you are offered all three, you are likely to be getting something that is too good to be true. "Quick" usually means now, but for most suppliers it means additional cost. "Good" can mean high quality, but will usually come at greater cost. "Cheap" may be possible, but the quality may suffer and the speed may not be as quick as you need.

There are many things in life you can obtain quick and cheap. Take the hamburger: the quality is not going to be that of a prime steak, despite what the marketing might suggest. You can get a great first-class airline seat immediately (good and quick) but it will cost you more. You can get a beautiful garden if you plant and tend it yourself at a reasonable price, but it might take a year or two for the benefits to arrive. These three dynamics of value fit together in the same way as risk and benefit go hand in hand in that one will nearly always affect the other. For instance, if you want low risk you expect the cost to rise because low risk comes at a price. Similarly, if you are prepared to take greater risk you will probably be offered better returns.

What do we mean by total value?

In most negotiations there is a central issue. This might relate to the price of an office lease, a trade union challenging changes to working practices, or an internal negotiation over who gets what percentage of the marketing budget, for example. Whatever the issue, this provides you with an opportunity to better negotiate around it by introducing and trading it against other related variables, considerations, and implications, all of which will have some bearing on the total value.

A GREAT PRICE CAN OFTEN LEAD TO A LOUSY DEAL

Anyone who drives price as the only consideration is likely to end up with regrets if they accept the mantra "you get what you pay for." Effective negotiators will use power derived from time and circumstance, the power resulting from supply and demand and from the available options that one party or the other has. How much you understand about these and how much you decide you use them will be down to your judgment. Where there is some level of dependency in play once the deal is done (as in most B2B situations), then total value carries a greater consequence than simply price. If you feel comfortable booking laser eye surgery or a vasectomy at the lowest price then you have to come to terms with the risk you take at a very personal level. Would you hire the cheapest lawyer to manage your divorce or send your kids to the cheapest dentist because of price? Probably not. There will be many other variables in play and you will probably place a value on each of them.

Try to remove *price* as the main issue of contention. It is the most transparent and contentious of issues ("what you get, I lose and what I get, you lose"), especially when dealt with in isolation. Indeed, even if you negotiate creatively around a range of variables but leave price until the end, you are likely to finish up back at 4 o'clock – hard bargaining. With nowhere to go you are just as likely to deadlock over price at the end as if this had been the only issue under consideration. By introducing it early instead, you can always revisit it as part of changing other terms during the negotiation. Keep it in the mix, and conditional.

Total value comes not only from the basic terms agreed, but also from certainty or whether the deal will actually deliver the value intended over the lifetime of the agreement.

Where you are reliant on the other party's motivation to deliver over the lifetime of the agreement, to perform or comply, and in the event that their performance falters, you or your business will be exposed to the implications of such shortfalls. So part of your consideration needs to focus on the period of time known as "follow through." This means setting out terms to protect and ensure adequate compensation in the case of lack of compliance or performance. These terms should also ensure that the consequences to you are addressed and compensated for, removing the need for further negotiations. Essentially you are "future proofing" the agreement.

THE SIX PRIMARY VARIABLES

There are six primary variables that tend to feature across any type of deal from business to politics. This helps to capture all the issues that are likely to affect the total value of your agreements. Once defined, you can use them to broaden out the scope of the agreement and to consider the consequences of performance around each of these variables. During your planning this also provides you with the opportunity to introduce a range of conditions linked to each variable.

1. **Price, fee, or margin** (how much will be paid).
2. **Volume** (how many, how much, or what types).
3. **Delivery** (when, where, response times).
4. **Contract period** (when it will start, how long it will run for, under what circumstances it will or can be terminated, when it will be reviewed, etc).
5. **Payment terms** (when, how, currency, etc).
6. **Specification** (what the product, service, or agreement will include, the quality, or how it will be supported).

1. Price, fee, or margin

You can build agreements that feature differing pricing structures. These can be linked to issues such as:

- the purpose for which the product or service is to be used;
- geography (regional pricing to be used and by whom); and
- relationship loyalty.

They should also be linked directly to the other five primary variables. If this is not done, then the transparency involving "what I get, you lose and what you get, I lose" will usually result in tough positional bargaining. So try wherever possible to link price with other issues.

2. Volume

There are few cases where volume does not feature in negotiations and in most cases there is a direct relationship between price and volume, unless you are buying a one-off event or specific tangible item. The economies of scale usually provide for this, so much so that some businesses will reflect such a relationship on a published discount tariff. As an extension to the price list, this is also designed in an attempt to preempt further negotiation. Volume thresholds can sometimes be linked to retrospective discounts (a discount you receive on the whole order, but only when a certain volume order has been achieved) or can provide increased discount levels, depending on volume levels to promote loyalty and volume orders.

3. Delivery

This refers to where, by when, and how the physical product or services are to be delivered or completed.

Where delivery is stipulated to be by the end of the month, for example, further variables can be introduced to stipulate the consequences of not meeting these delivery commitments. This can take the form of a penalty clause, or other forms of compensation linked to protecting against implications in the event that commitments are not met.

The construction industry uses this approach where contractors have to finish within certain timelines to enable others to start work. If they do not, there are financial implications for both the main contractor and other sub-contractors. So the risk and consequences are negotiated into the agreement so that responsibility and implications around timescales sit with the sub-contractor. They in turn may choose to negotiate terms that accommodate shared risk, recognizing circumstances beyond their control like weather:

"If it rains for more than 50% of the days we have to complete the job, we will be allowed a further 10 days to complete without penalty."

4. Contract period

Think of the contract duration. The start, stop, pause, cancel, re-commence terms, each with different circumstances attached, and you can start to imagine just how many variables could be included when you consider contract period. For those involved in negotiating lease contracts, this is one of the most valuable variables, in that to attract a 5-year agreement rather than a 1-year agreement buys so much more security and certainty.

Even if it is a rolling contract (ongoing) there will still be circumstances upon which an opt-out clause can be contractually exercised. Another variable designed to protect contract period commitments is termination, where you stipulate where one party can terminate the contract with or without reason or consequence as well as defining when the option to renew becomes available.

5. Payment terms

There are so many ways of constructing payment terms to reflect the risk to those involved, the commitment to see the work through, or simply to increase the value of the deal. They can be broken down to include:

- when and how payment will be made;
- advanced deposits;
- phased payments;
- even circumstances where delayed payment may be acceptable; and
- late payment penalties.

Proposals that include payment terms can be triggered based on performance, can be held on account, paid retrospectively, be refundable, or with a defined number of days credit.

Sometimes payment terms are a reflection of cash flow requirements, the risks associated with the creditworthiness or history of the other party, or simply a reflection of the standard terms of the dominant party in the negotiation.

Whichever one of these features, payment terms have a financial implication for both parties and will feature as a primary variable.

6. Specification

Specification relates to almost anything that affects the quality of the product or service being offered. As a simple illustration, the materials specification of a garment in addition to design can relate to size, fabric, wash type, buttons, zips, lining, finishing, presentation, and packaging; and each of these will have a multitude of options each impacting on the cost or value of the finished product. Imagine the number of variables involved for a company sourcing aircraft from one of the main manufacturers with literally thousands of specifications, which all affect the total outcome of the agreement. The complexity of the product or service, where it is being sourced from, the financing arrangements, and the relationships involved will all have some impact on the level of detail and the number of variables that will relate to specification.

WORKING WITH VARIABLES

Whenever the focus and pressure is on price, there is a tendency to re-negotiate other variables as part of offsetting any implications on price movement. This usually involves introducing other variables as part of compensation for or adjusting the price point. This enables the Complete Skilled Negotiator to maintain the total value on offer despite price pressures. In other words, this is about moving the package around to reduce risk and to grow the total value. Everything is conditional – which allows you to protect the value – so if one variable needs adjusting down others can be moved to offset the implications.

NEGOTIATING FOR WHAT IS IMPORTANT TO YOU

A leading recruitment consultancy specializing in senior appointments offered as standard to its clients to replace appointees if they were to leave their employment within 3 months. In the interest of good relations, they had been known to extend this period as they were prepared to take some responsibility, having shortlisted the candidate.

(Continued)

(*Continued*)

Six months into his employment the Creative Director of media company M1G was "let go" on the basis of cultural fit. The senior nature of the role meant that he had spent his first 3 months in the business in induction. It took 3 more months before the board understood that his disruptive nature was not healthy for the business and took the decision to terminate his contract. At this time they called their contact at the recruitment consultancy to discuss next steps.

HR Director of M1G Mary Donaldson held a meeting with the representative of the recruitment consultancy to explain the considerable cost incurred. This included salary, expenses, recruitment fees, and notice period, which altogether topped £250,000 in what had turned out to be a poor fit.

The recruitment partner explained his terms and said he was keen to help M1G to find the right creative director. Mary went on to highlight the fact that they had used their services three times a year each year for the past 2 years to attract top talent in various posts. The partner said that he would re-examine volume discount structure for the following year.

Mary adjourned the meeting and considered her agenda and the planning that she had done to date. Risk had become an important issue, as was the value that the eventual successful quality candidate might bring. She returned a week later and tabled a proposal that included a "12-month, replace for free" clause in return for the standard placement rate, plus a further 20% if the candidate achieved all of their performance objectives in year 1. It was a model she had seen work well in the sports world where team players' fees are often based on number of performances, goals, or country representations. By re-packing the variables to reflect the priorities of her company, she was also able to negotiate a 50% discount on the original replacement.

KNOWING WHAT VARIABLES YOU HAVE TO WORK WITH

Your planning and preparation should help you to create more value from your agreements starting with expanding the issues and variables available.

It's easier to visualize the need to plan when creating something with a physical form, such as an aircraft, compared with planning simply to build an agreement. You can more easily imagine the design and planning needed when creating a new aircraft, critical to it ever coming together, let alone flying, in the first place. The creativity employed by an artist, starting with a blank canvas and with all the work to do ahead of them, requires flexibility and a mental picture for what will be. In both cases, options and creativity play a significant part in ensuring a successful outcome, as well as necessity for some visionary thought.

During the planning phase, scoping and taking the opportunity to create value starts with understanding the options and bringing together component parts or variables that will make the deal both possible and ultimately more valuable.

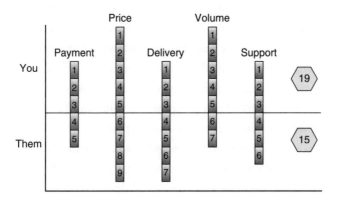

Figure 9.1 Trading off variables.

Moving conditional proposals or variables around, changing who takes responsibility for what, and shifting performance triggers, discount thresholds, performance conditions, and contract terms in your negotiations is essentially about you establishing the point where both parties will and can agree.

Attaching triggers to variables

Most variables can be used on a sliding scale. For example, if you are discussing volume, the order could be anything from 1 to 1 million, which would in turn affect other variables.

However, volume can be linked to a trigger that sets off other terms you agree. For example, once you have ordered 1000 the 5% discount commences, or if you are able to place an order for 10,000 in any given month the delivery becomes free, or by agreeing to the total order now we will allow you to draw off stock as you require it over the next 6 months. Each condition serves as a trigger that, if met, provides for the benefit offered.

Triggers can be applied to any variable and serve to motivate the behaviors of the other party as well as to protect your interests. Variables can also have triggers attached to them that relate to a particular performance, beyond or up to which another condition is met. For example, a discount that kicks in after the order for the first 200 has been received. The 200th order represents the trigger for the discount to become applicable. The payment terms can only be offered following receipt of the 20% deposit. Receipt of the full deposit is the trigger for the payment terms to be applicable. Terms are linked to a performance threshold (an order of 200), where further commitments then become applicable.

Once you have commenced your negotiation, you can trade off variables gradually, use absolute triggers, and adapt trigger thresholds (performance levels) depending on what you want to achieve. With any variable, you can:

- adjust it;
- link it;
- place a trigger on it; or
- even move it bit by bit.

This is commonly known as **the "salami" tactic.** As an example of trading off a variable gradually, you could link a quicker guaranteed response on the service provided conditional of a reduction in payment terms from 45 days to 40 days. You may trade a commitment

to flexible delivery timings in return for a further move of payment terms to 36 days. Perhaps you have the knowledge that they are really keen to get their 30 days payment agreed, which is their "symbol of success." So you go back and finally offer them the 30 days in return for a shorter termination notice period. Each time, you are attracting more value (or less risk by your calculation) than the very 15 days payment terms that you expected to move to in the first place. By this time you may have calculated that, although the 15 days have cost you the equivalent of 0.5% on the deal, the concessions you have attracted are worth 1.1%.

RISK AS A NEGOTIABLE

Even if a partnership relationship existed, based on an aligned strategy, how do you reasonably ensure that you remain continuously aligned as both your companies continue to reassess their strategies?

In other words, when considering the future and the contract you are about to sign, never assume a constant state. Things will always change over time. Performance, reliability, the market, and demand can and usually do change, and should challenge your assumptions about how profitable the deal is, will be, or has been. It is these very issues driven by change that you need to factor into your planning. The value to you of a guarantee that protects you against change, and the value of accountability and responsibility are often not the same as the cost of accepting them.

For example, the price or value of a flexible airline ticket will mean different things to you and the airline in the transaction; for example, the convenience of being able to switch and change can provide tremendous value to you. Imagine if you are having difficulty getting home from a business meeting late on a Friday night following a flight cancellation. Yet the absolute cost to the airline of offering a flexible service in many cases is negligible. So how much is this protection against change or the cost of inconvenience following change worth to you? Again, that depends on your circumstances. Creative negotiators understand how to use convenience and flexibility, and choose to build even greater levels of "total value" into their agreements starting from inside the head of the other party.

Where it is difficult to estimate or agree on risk, insurance also plays its part as a variable in negotiation. By insuring yourself or the other party against certain risks or insisting that they take out policies to protect against risks you can overcome some of the more challenging aspects of uncertainty.

You may not think twice about insuring your own contents in your house because of the known risks, or insuring your house from damage as for many it is their greatest asset. Equally, many people insure their health, their car (because the law says they have to), even their washing machine, just in case it stops working. Insuring against the possible and in some cases probable is a further variable that can be used for accounting for risks. This same thought process is used as part of a negotiator's thinking as they identify ways of agreeing to terms whilst balancing the risks involved.

"In the event that you fail to meet the payment schedule, we reserve the right to reclaim the stock, or we will insure you against non-payment." The premium will be built into the overall pricing structure. Either way you mitigate against the risk, which is agreed as part of the negotiation based on the level of risk you see in play.

Protecting the value

This involves protecting the value you think you have created in your agreement. What if delivery, specification, or payment terms are not adhered to? What are the implications to you and how do you protect against them within the terms agreed? Negotiating risk first involves identifying the risks which could prevent the contract delivering what it's supposed to, and ensuring that the terms of the agreement reflect those risks to both parties.

Risks come in many forms and are often overlooked, as they do not necessarily reflect immediately on the profit and loss sheet. Ask any bank selling mortgages between 2004 and 2009. Ignore risk at your peril. Better still, trade it creatively against each of the primary variables. Insurance companies treat risk as a defined tangible issue and so should those of us buying or selling tangible products or services.

Accountability

Once risks are identified, you can focus on who will take, insure, mitigate against, or accept liability for the risks. Your next step involves building into your proposals a basis upon which the risks will be accommodated or compensated for. One challenge or opportunity – depending on how you see it – comes from understanding both parties' attitude to risk. If you have had a particularly bad experience in the past and the cost of putting it right still resonates, your attitude towards protecting against it and the value you associate with such cover may be greater than the cost implications for the other party providing it.

The guarantees provided with a second-hand car bought from a main dealer will have some value for which we accept that there will be a premium built into the price compared with buying privately. Many will regard this premium as a price worth paying. They are buying out the risk, buying confidence in that what they are paying is the maximum total price following any issues they may have with the car over the guaranteed period. They are buying certainty and for that they are prepared to pay. The way each party interprets the level of risk, or even the severity of that risk, often varies based on their own circumstances and those individuals involved in the decision making on their behalf.

Risk is different for different people

In the same way that supply and demand, and time and circumstances serve to set the balance of power in negotiations, risk and reward provide us with the basis for weighing up investment opportunities. Different industries have different tools for assessing risk and placing a premium on it, to hedge against it or to insure against it. In some cases where the deal is of strategic importance they may even be prepared to accept some degree of uncertainty. Dealing with uncertainty over the long term may represent a good bet given the potential value at stake. Risk as a variable is not bad or to be avoided, it just needs to be recognized, understood, and managed. Whether you are a private equity firm buying into a business, negotiating for mining rights, or buying computer chips from Korea, risk will feature in your considerations and the terms you agree.

In the field of litigation, for example, how do you place a cost or value on the risk or benefit of negotiating an out-of-court settlement? How does a PR company view the implications of risk associated with bad PR exposure and the degree to which this could affect their reputation, versus the legal costs of defending one's reputation? It is probably too late to insure against such risks so you need to remain as objective as possible, set your break points and get inside the other party's head. Each case will be unique and can only be assessed by those facing the consequences.

Managing compliance and performance?

If you missed your mortgage payment this month, your lender would want the outstanding payment at the earliest moment. They would also insist on charging further interest on the late payment. This same philosophy or consideration should exist with any agreement where risks are to be addressed. Without this consideration you may well find yourself involved with relationship issues through a lack of clarity around obligations where commitments are not met.

A useful way of exploring risk is to ask the question: "What would happen if …?"

- They do not meet their deadlines?
- The specification falls short?
- They want to terminate early?
- Their circumstances change?
- Our circumstances change and we need more flexibility?

- Exchange rates fluctuate wildly?
- Their key personnel leave?

And so on. There are so many possibilities relating to the potential for change, which many businesses are renowned for building into their "standard terms" in the small print. The reality is that these risks are two-way and wherever possible you should include them as part of your negotiation agenda.

PREPARING TO MANAGE COMPLEXITY

The shape of most deals, where a range of issues are involved, changes each time a new proposal is tabled. Changes in terms of total value happen throughout the negotiation until both parties agree to settle with a particular set of terms and conditions. The process provides a fluid situation, like watching shifting sands. The shape may get bigger or smaller, longer or shorter, fatter or thinner. This can make tracking the deal and the implications of changes difficult.

Building an agreement that entails a process involving many proposals is challenging because of the need to trade around specific variables whilst remaining mindful of the overall picture and total value implications.

For example, whilst negotiating an agreement that involves agreeing to guarantee that a job will be finished by the end of the month you may want to consider the things that you cannot control, such as circumstances that might make the commitment difficult to meet. These could be categorized by both parties as valid reasons for the job being delayed.

Exploring all possibilities

Other issues that will need resolving during your negotiations could also come at a price, so the concept of "nothing is agreed until everything is agreed" allows you to carefully explore all possibilities and agree in principle to ideas subject to all other conditions being agreeable. If necessary you can take proposals back off the table in the event that conditions discussed latterly are not agreed or the overall deal becomes unacceptable. One danger to watch for as you explore possibilities is sending the other party signals regarding which issues you are prepared to agree to, or those that are of particular importance to you. It's OK to say yes to proposals in principle providing the other party is aware that any one proposal is subject to all other conditions being acceptable. With some trust, and the appropriate climate, the shape of the deal should be allowed to change and evolve. Most of the issues will be in some way inter-related because most will impact on the total cost or value.

I have heard of more challenging negotiations being compared with the building of a 10,000-piece jigsaw. First you group pieces together, perhaps edges, then you gather the pieces into color zones. Then you start to piece together sections of the picture, leaving some pieces not fitting, so you go off in search of the right piece so that you can continue. You need patience, persistence, and an eye for how the picture is coming together. You know you have enough pieces, it's just a matter of the sequence and matching that's needed. With a jigsaw you have a picture forming, providing instant feedback on your progress. In negotiation you only have the response of the other party to rely on, but the way you approach the task has many similarities. With a jigsaw, however, the next piece may or may not fit. In negotiation a proposal that was rejected earlier may be accepted later under different circumstances. With a jigsaw you know it's possible from the outset as you have the right number of pieces at the start to finish the task. In negotiation there is no such certainty, whereas with a jigsaw there is one outcome that is as predictable as the picture is on the box. In negotiation, the shape of the deal can and usually does vary depending on how the negotiators have responded to each other's ideas and positions.

Taking your time and being patient
Working on the deal does not mean that each proposal should be met with approval, rejection, or even a counter proposal. Some ideas need more work and time to consider before you can even respond to them. Be prepared to park issues that you can come back to later.

Where the number of variables makes the negotiation complex, you should (subject to time constraints) take the time to adjourn and consider the possibilities. When you are in need of further authorization or stakeholder buy-in, take the time to consult before responding. This is especially the case if your ideas are new or include less tangible issues such as flexibility, convenience, or risk.

Being open to new ideas

Flexibility not only increases the chances of your performance being more productive, but will also throw up new ideas for consideration that you might otherwise have filtered out very early on through being too single-minded or focused.

- If sustainable profit growth is the endgame, then allow yourself to explore how this can come about and make the time to do this.
- If you are involved in a conflict resolution negotiation, there may be a range of options available to you that achieve the same end, each with its own merits.
- If agreement to a "change in working practices" with the trade unions is what you are faced with, there will be a range of options available, each of which may facilitate an acceptance of change.

There is often more than one way to achieve your end result so try to remain focused on building solutions even where there is ambiguity or irrational behavior in play. The next time you feel the need for a quick resolution and find yourself considering compromises, ask yourself: "Am I buying myself certainty in obtaining an early commitment and effectively buying myself some 'comfort,' or should I make more time and be patient with the process?"

Agreeing in principle

Throughout your discussions you've agreed to nothing until the end. Of course, this could result in you sending the wrong messages and signals if you appear too open to ideas that are clearly not acceptable. Your attitude and response should remain balanced and, where necessary, point out how challenging some areas will be to entertain. Slow down and provide yourself time to think things through. Examine the "what ifs" and adopt a mindset of "how" and "under what circumstances," rather than "no," "can't," or "won't," which are so easy to adopt when you can't see the total picture.

Changing the shape of the deal – repackaging
Creative negotiators avoid deadlock by identifying ways of changing the shape of the deal, which allows the other party to move. They do this whilst at the same time moving the value of the deal forward for themselves. The more you understand about the other party's position and points of interest, the more obvious this becomes.

Try to focus on what you can do, move your instinctive attitude from "blame" or "defend" to "qualify," and then build solution-based proposals. Problem solving is far more rewarding and sustainable than seeking simply to drive down their terms.

FOCUS ON THE PROBLEM, NOT ON THE PEOPLE

Marketing events coordinator Cuprinord specializes in marketing business forums on cruise ships. This involves hundreds of company executives who pay premium prices to attend the forum, which involves about 30 prescreened meetings with potential vendors. Cuprinord charter the ships out of New York, Houston, Southampton, and Sydney for an annual 3-day, all-inclusive event from the cruise company Banasik. Each event accommodates 250 potential purchasers and 400 paying guests who get to meet for 45 minutes with the best business match for their services over the 3 days. For each event Cuprinord pays a $2m advance deposit with a further $4m payable within 6 weeks of the event. It was the second year of trading between them, with the first four events having been a success.

Typically the ship would arrive 2 days before the event in order for a full clean and service to take place. Banasik knew this was tight but had adopted it as part of their business model.

Five days before the event was due to run on October 3, the CEO of Cuprinord received a call from the COO of Banasik. He was advised of the extreme weather conditions in the Gulf of Mexico and that their ship, the Beauty would not arrive in Houston until two days later than scheduled. This placed the entire event in jeopardy.

Following a heated conversation, Cuprinord considered handing the event over to their legal team and implementing a cancellation communication to all concerned. Banasik recognized that, despite weather being an "act of God," the loss of earnings, reputation, and future earnings lawsuit that could follow required swift action. If it was proven that their allowance for such events was not reasonable for the time of year, there would be potential consequences given their contractual responsibilities.

The situation was destined to be a lose–lose outcome. The COO of Banasik pulled together with his team a proposal that started a 3-hour problem-solving negotiation. It involved commencing the event from Miami where the Beauty could dock on September 30. To offer flight travel, accommodation, and if necessary charter flights from Houston to Miami, return, and finally a call center provision for handling the 24-hour communication exercise that would follow. Needless to say, there were 27 other variables that came into play, but after 3 hours an agreement was forged, which not only enabled the event to run, but preserved the working relationship between the companies involved.

PLANNING FROM A PRACTICAL PERSPECTIVE

I have saved what is probably the most important element of negotiation until the end. It is then both easy to find as a reference and to share with others. If preparation is critical to negotiation then preparing in a team, as a team, using the same thinking, language, and approach is just as important as the act itself (see Chapter 7, under "Empowerment within team roles").

This approach, consisting of a number of tools, provides a standard for preparation that is easy to utilize and delivers consistency, confidence, and certainty. It also ensures that you are thinking from inside the head of the other party in the way that you evaluate the importance and value of variables, and build an agenda aimed at maximizing value. The beauty of the planning process is that you can start with your primary variables, of price, volume, timescales and contract length, specification, and payment terms. Your planning can then move on to examining the hidden costs.

Your first challenge is the discipline required to make the time and use it productively to plan through your negotiation. Some lack the belief that preparation will really pay off. Another challenge could be that in the past there has been a lack of a clear or respected process that has proved to deliver results, which can also dampen motivation. There are always other things you could be doing with your time but rarely one that will provide you with such certainty, alignment, and confidence for your negotiation as a well-thought-through plan.

Planning is by its nature proactive and where you make the time to work through the possibilities you have already gained an advantage before entering the negotiating room.

The process

To help simplify the scoping and planning process we have created a number of basic pro formas, which fit logically together and have been used by hundreds of businesses globally for their negotiation planning.

The aim of the negotiation planning tools is to help you scope the potential of your deal, work out the relative values, plan out your initial proposals, and then monitor the value of your agreement as discussions unfold.

Tool	Purpose
Trade-storming (honeycomb) ↓	Helps you to brainstorm potential issues
Trade surveyor ↓	Helps you to prioritize low-cost/high-value trades
Issue map ↓	Helps you to link and group relationships between tradable issues
Agenda* ↓	Helps you to structure and gain clarity before and during the negotiation
Move planner* ↓	Helps you to define initial specific conditional details
Record of offers*	Helps you to record and track proposals throughout the negotiation process

*Operational tools used during the negotiation

Figure 9.2 Planning tools.

Trade-storming

The first step in the planning process is commonly known as brain-storming; we call it trade-storming. It is the starting point from which you may want to involve other stakeholders to pool ideas or to challenge any assumptions.

This tool is represented by a simple honeycomb model. It invites you to list each of the issues that you believe will feature as part of your pending negotiation, and then start to identify potential connections or relationships between them. These are not always obvious to start with, which is why this tool is useful in helping you to visualize as you think through and expand on the more obvious variables. The Complete Skilled Negotiator will develop several variables using the trade-storming tool as they consider how each variable can become linked or grouped by association with other variables. Delivery may be one variable but, when you start to consider the issues that sit around delivery and are worthy of negotiation, you could list timing, venues, response times, accuracy, regularity, and so on. All will have some bearing on the value or cost associated with this element of the agreement.

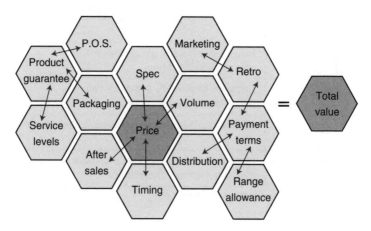

Figure 9.3 Trade-storming.

Trade surveyor

Ultimately you will need to form some initial conditional proposals for your meeting. Having worked through the variables most likely to feature on your agenda, your next job is then to work out the relative values involved for you and the other party.

This means categorizing each variable according to the interests, priorities, and values the other party places on them. It is an opportunity to compare the relative cost and benefit values involved from both parties' perspectives. For this we use a pro forma known as a trade surveyor. It's useful to use this as part of your exploration meetings with the other party. During the discussions, you can qualify any assumptions that you may have on the value that they place on each issue.

Issues	Take		Give	
	Value to us	Cost to them	Cost to us	Value to them
Price	High	High	High	High
Volume discount			Medium	High
Promotion fees			Low	High
Payment terms			Low	High
Distribution	High	Low		
Volumes	High	Low		
Promotions	High	Low		
Exclusivity			Low	High

Rate: High/Medium/Low   For the purpose of examining possibilities

Figure 9.4 Trade surveyor.

Building value in negotiation relies partly on trading low-cost variables in return for high-value variables. The trade surveyor helps you identify the variables that provide you (or both parties) with an incremental gain. This approach provides a useful way of understanding the most likely value relationships in play and should help inform you when developing conditional proposals prior to your meeting. Because of a lack of transparency, win–win usually means that one party wins (gains more value), but that the other party wins more. In other words, it's not about the fair, equitable 50–50 sharing of value as the term win–win might suggest. It is simply a process that attracts the interests of both parties because of the potential benefits available, however this might be split; and conditional trading is central to this.

Issue map

We use the issue map to visually work through the relative low-cost, high-value relationships and examine the different ways in which any one variable can be coupled with others, as part of building initial, conditional proposals.

Depending on the relative values you place on each variable, you can use the issue map to explore possible linkages. You may link price to volume or payment terms to delivery scheduling, and so on. This is only a basic way of playing with possibilities, but it allows you to consider different options before constructing specific proposals.

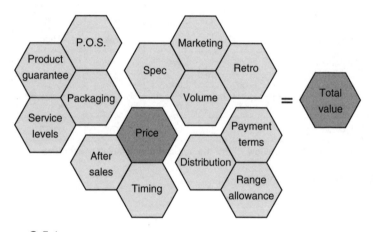

Figure 9.5 Issue map.

On your issue map you may, for example:

- draw a line for your own reference to indicate a potential coupling between price and volume; and
- draw a line to couple price and specification as you weigh up the best way of linking issues.

Using your trade surveyor, you can start to draw potential links between each of the variables. You can start to visualize how they may be coupled for the purpose of constructing proposals.

Agenda

Having qualified the variables, it's time to pull together and communicate an agenda – preferably one that you can both agree on and that will provide the basis and parameters for discussions.

The one benefit of a qualified agenda is that you know what has been tabled and what is outstanding. Say you have worked through the timescales, costings, and quality but know from the agenda that contract length and payment terms are outstanding issues. You would still have plenty of scope to negotiate even if that means bringing timescales back on to the table by linking them to contract length. You can address unacceptable terms by linking them to proposals that are yet to be tabled. It can feel very open-ended at first, but by leaving flexibility around some of the issues as discussions evolve, you can discuss more openly and, depending on the level of trust, explore different options. Of course, there will be tension and positions in play that you will need to manage, so just remember to ensure that your position at any point in time is conditional and clearly linked.

AGENDA

1. Service and quality specification
2. Information and data sharing
3. Volume ordering
4. Fee structure
5. Discount levels
6. Commencement date
7. Contract period
8. Payment terms
9. Confidentiality

Figure 9.6 Sample agenda.

A mutually agreed agenda to work from can help you to manage some initial ambiguity and will help build trust. A comprehensive agenda provides a list of those issues that need to be agreed, giving everyone involved transparency. The idea of agreeing to one issue without everything else being lined up can feel exposing, and is the one area of ambiguity that you will have to accommodate.

The move planner

The move planner is used to detail the specific conditional terms against each of the trade-offs you plan to make, providing you with a list of well-thought-through proposals.

Each proposal needs to be specific, allowing the other party the chance to calculate, weigh, consider, and respond. It is no help to simply ask for improved payment terms in return for a higher-volume order. You have to be more specific. If not, you can't reasonably expect them to take the offer seriously or be able to respond to it. If it's 60 days for a 10% increase, say so. Detail it on your move planner. It is the one place to record your proposals in advance of discussions. They are the conditions that you have thought through, calculated, and considered objectively in the cold light of day.

Move Planner

If you...	Then we...
Distribution 500	Price £14.90
Volume 1m	Volume discount 1.5%
Volume 1.3m Promotions 6	Marketing investment £80k

Figure 9.7 Move planner.

Before you start to make any proposals, qualify their priorities one last time. It is amazing how these can change over relatively short periods of time.

"Last week you told me that delivery by week 12 would work for you, now you are saying week 8. Just how important is week 8?"

Understanding how they value things right now is critical. I have seen people in negotiations trying to negotiate for what they think they want, rather than for what they actually need. Your questioning should be aimed at qualifying what they *need*.

Imagine a construction manager who insists on the scaffolding being removed from the construction site with 1 day's notice. He regards it as critical. The hire company is able to accommodate the request but will charge a premium for a quick response. When the builder is questioned, it comes to light that his construction contract states that he has 7 days to clear the site. Seven days' notice will save him a 5% premium on the scaffold rental. It's not dissimilar to price. Most people think they want a better price but often it's a better deal or enhanced value that they really seek.

When tabling a conditional proposal, at first try to avoid introducing more than three items at once. It can prove difficult for the other party to calculate or respond to the proposal in any meaningful way. It also slows down any momentum created. If you table every conditional proposal you have prepared all at once, you are more likely to draw a blank or a delayed response from the other party for three reasons.

1. They will find it incredibly difficult under pressure to calculate what it all means. Therefore, they are likely to only pick off the terms they do like, whilst ignoring the conditions attached to them.
2. They are left with the task of working out links or connections between each conditional proposal, which will potentially confuse them further still.
3. They will have some ideas that you might want to weigh up before tabling your entire position.

This approach of gradually tabling your proposals and allowing the deal to build requires patience and a certain degree of comfort with early ambiguity.

To start with, neither party will be able to see the whole deal and yet may be asked to respond to part of it. Remember, where there is complexity, you may need to park elements and come back to them later, having examined some of the other agenda points first.

The record of offers

This is especially important when you are dealing with many variables and you need to maintain a clear record of progress. Negotiators are often found scribbling notes in no particular order as the deal unfolds. Before long, you can barely make sense of the notes, or what the other party has suggested, let alone the last full position tabled. The "record of offers" table allows you to record all positions and movement, enabling you to keep track of where you are up to and how you got there.

Issue	Yours	Theirs	Yours	Theirs	Yours	Theirs
Price/case	£14.90	£12.20	£14.50	£13.00		£13.60
Volume discount	1.5%	2.0%	1.75%	2.0%		
Marketing investment	£80,000	£150,000		£100,000		
Payment terms	30	60	60			
Distribution	500	400		500		
Volumes/pa	1,000,000	1,000,000	1,300,000	1,500,000		
Promotions	6	8	10	10		
Exclusivity	12 months	12 months				

Figure 9.8 Record of offers.

As you move across the page tracking your position with theirs, it allows you to summarize accurately and ensure that your facts are clear when you come to write up the agreement. Over time the record of offers allows you to:

- monitor the size of the moves they have made and on which variables; and
- summarize across the variables with your running total of your last position.

If you don't confirm what you have agreed to, how do you know what decisions were actually made? In many cases, this can lead to yet another negotiation later on.

Now you are ready to negotiate. The planning is done, the tactics understood, the behaviors tuned, and the thinking from inside their head in motion allowing you to see the deal opportunities as the other party sees them.

The Complete Skilled Negotiator is only as complete as their planning, and never so complete that they can take anything for granted. Never assuming, always enquiring. Never rushed, always considered and respectful. It's a tough balance requiring nerve, confidence, and tenacity, and it is for this reason that you can never afford to be complacent.

KEY TAKEAWAYS
- Without preparation before you enter the "negotiation arena," all the theory in the world (and indeed in this book!) will add up to nothing.
- Map out all the possible variables and value each from inside the other party's head.
- Focus on the potential total value of your agreement.
- Identify ways you can change the shape of the deal, which allows the other party to move, in order to build solution-based proposals rather than seeking to simply drive down their terms.
- There are six primary variables that feature across most deals (price, payment, timing, specification, volume, delivery), which, once defined, can be used to introduce a range of risk-based conditions that you can link to each variable.
- Use the six negotiation planning tools to help scope the potential of your deal, work out the relative values, plan out your initial proposals, and then monitor the value of your agreement as your discussions unfold.

Final Thoughts

Your ability to build agreements, dissolve deadlock situations, pre-condition expectations, and close sustainable deals requires all of the skills, attributes, knowledge, and self-awareness we have covered in *The Negotiation Book*.

For many, the challenges presented by negotiation do not come naturally and, as with any performance coupled with your own motivation to continuously improve, you have one of the most rewarding personal development opportunities available to you.

Negotiating effectively is firstly about accepting that it is only you who can influence the situations you are faced with. You can blame the market, personalities, timing, your options, the power balance, or any circumstance that you may think happens to be working against you, but ultimately it is you who can turn around situations (including deadlock situations) into workable and profitable deals.

It is time to stay calm, see the tactics for what they are, be proactive, and exercise nerve and patience. Power, real or perceived, however generated, will play its part in your negotiations. No matter how good you are as a negotiator, where the balance of power is against you or your circumstances, you will no doubt experience the frustration of feeling compromised. Trust your instinct, exercise composure. It will make the difference between the agreements where you create value and the ones where you simply distribute it.

If you have to take a time-out, adjourn the meeting, or go back and revisit the options, the fact that you recognize this and are prepared to take the time necessary is an indication that you are now behaving in an appropriate and conscious manner.

Know what you are trying to achieve and always try to work out what they are trying to achieve. This requires clarity in purpose and an acceptance, for those who are competitive in nature, that negotiation is not about winning, it is about optimizing value, and to do this you must see the deal as they do.

Taking control of any situation requires planning and never is this as true as in negotiation. Negotiators who find themselves reacting to their environment and situation tend to place themselves in weaker positions than necessary. Always try to be as proactive and prepared as possible. It is the one thing you can do to enhance your prospects.

Self-awareness is another dimension that differentiates the performance of the Complete Skilled Negotiator from others. They are not driven by fairness or consumed by their own ego. They and you should do that which is appropriate having weighed and considered each set of circumstances you are faced with.

To listen, think and reflect, and to understand those around you and then consciously apply those skills we have learned is what hopefully I have been able to promote and explain in *The Negotiation Book*.

Negotiation is like no other skill. I know from my experience, as well as that of my team, my clients, and my family, that it can offer huge and well-earned rewards for anyone ready to become the Complete Skilled Negotiator.

About The Gap Partnership

FREE EXCLUSIVE ONLINE NEGOTIATION PROFILER

Continue your journey to becoming a Complete Skilled Negotiator with The Gap Partnership's free and exclusive online negotiator profiler.

Through a series of highly targeted questions, the negotiation profiler will assess where your own individual strengths and development needs as a negotiator lie whilst measuring your negotiation knowledge and understanding against those of the fourteen behaviors presented in The Negotiation Book. Once you have completed the negotiation profiler you will receive recommend tailored suggestions for your own further negotiation development.

www.thegappartnership.com/negotiationprofiler

ABOUT THE GAP PARTNERSHIP

The Gap Partnership is a global negotiation consultancy working with over 500 blue chip organizations from offices around the world. Founded in 1997, we specialize exclusively in negotiation. We've studied it, dissected it, analyzed it and applied it. It's a business discipline we are passionate about. All our consultants are negotiation practitioners; all have real-world commercial and negotiation experience.

At The Gap Partnership we understand that it is human nature, not businesses, that so often influences and underpins the potential for negotiation agreements. Only by getting inside the other person's head can we start to negotiate effectively.

www.thegappartnership.com

NEGOTIATION DEVELOPMENT PROGRAMS

At The Gap Partnership we have a comprehensive proposition that provides a framework for all negotiation development program needs. All our programs are highly flexible to meet our individual Clients' needs. Our product team are dedicated to ensuring that all Clients receive the right solution for their teams and businesses.

The Complete Skilled Negotiator

The most effective experiential negotiation behavior change program in the world.

The Essential Negotiator

Provides a clear behavioral framework within an experiential program based on the fundamentals of negotiation enabling attendees to structure, plan and perform more effectively.

The Creative Negotiator

Designed for those who negotiate multi-issue agreements with long-term business partners and require a collaborative approach to negotiation.

The Strategic Negotiator

Provides a thorough understanding and process framework which helps our Clients and their teams proactively plan, control and perform in more complex negotiations.

For more information on our consulting and negotiation development programs please visit us at www.thegappartnership.com.

At The Gap Partnership we deliver negotiation development progams and in countries throughout the world. Please contact us if you would like to discuss how we can help you or your team become a Complete Skilled Negotiator.

UK
Ashlyns Hall
Chesham Road
Berkhamsted
Hertfordshire
HP4 2ST
UK
Tel +44 (0)1442 291900

GERMANY
Marc-Chagall-Strasse 2-6
40477 Düsseldorf
Deutschland
Tel +49 (0)211 440 3890

USA
411 Theodore Fremd Ave
Suite 230, Rye
New York
NY 10580
USA
Tel +1 914 925 0380

SOUTH AFRICA
25 Highwick Avenue
Kenilworth
7708 Cape Town
South Africa
Tel +27 (0) 217610576

HONG KONG
Room 901
Lee Garden One
33 Hysan Avenue
Causeway Bay
Hong Kong
香港銅鑼灣希慎道33號利園一期9樓901室
Tel +852 3796 3631

AUSTRALIA
Suite 103, 221 Miller Street
North Sydney 2060
Australia
Tel +61 (0) 2 8937 0299

Index